FROM GIRDLE MAKER TO WATER COMMISSIONER

THE GREAT GILDERSLEEVE

THE PIONEERING SPIN-OFF PROGRAM THAT MADE BROADCAST HISTORY!

KRISTINE OHKUBO

Copyright © 2024 by Kristine Ohkubo.

All rights reserved. No part of this publication may be reproduced, distributed, or transmitted in any form or by any means, including photocopying, recording, or other electronic or mechanical methods, without the prior written permission of the author, except in the case of brief quotations embodied in critical reviews and certain other noncommercial uses permitted by copyright law. For permission requests, contact the author using the website address provided below.

https://kristineohkubo.wixsite.com/non-fiction-author

From Girdle Maker to Water Commissioner-The Great Gildersleeve/Kristine Ohkubo. —1st ed.

ISBN 979-8-3302-8862-5

Acknowledgements

I would like to express my heartfelt gratitude to Mrs. Mary Anna Waterman for entrusting and befriending a novice writer many years ago who had a deep passion for creating a book centered around a beloved old-time radio show, *The Great Gildersleeve*.

Mary Anna was married to Willard Waterman, the actor who assumed the role of the Great Gildersleeve on NBC (National Broadcasting Company) after Harold Peary's departure, for an impressive fifty-eight years. During our conversations, she captivated me with her fascinating stories and played a crucial role in helping me gather the essential information that laid the groundwork for my manuscript.

I also wish to express my appreciation to Chuck Schaden, the broadcaster, historian, and host of the program *Those Were the Days*. He not only provided me with the missing tapes of the show for me to listen to, but also invited me as a guest on the program to discuss my book during its creation stages.

Throughout the years, numerous individuals have provided assistance and support to me, including the members of SPERDVAC (The Society to Preserve and Encourage Radio Drama, Variety and Comedy), the Gassman brothers, Tim Hollis, Jerry Haendiges, and several others that I am unable to mention due to space constraints.

I am deeply grateful for each and every one of you. I've continued my efforts to have this book published, fueled by the unwavering support I have received.

i. Mr. and Mrs. Willard Waterman. Circa 1940s. Public domain.

Table of Contents

Introduction 1

Fibber McGee and Molly 7

79 Wistful Vista 9
Don Quinn 17
Throckmorton P. Gildersleeve 23

The Great Gildersleeve 27

From Wistful Vista to Parkside Avenue 29
    Characters and Cast 35
Leonard Levinson 37
Harold Peary 41
Willard Waterman 53
Walter Tetley 59
Lurene Tuttle 69
Louise Erickson 77
Mary Lee Robb 83
Lillian Randolph 89
Richard Crenna 95
Earle Ross 101
Richard LeGrand 107
Forrest Lewis 113
Arthur Q. Bryan 117
Shirley Mitchell 123

  Bea Benaderet 131

  Cathy Lewis 135

  Gale Gordon 141

  Jim Backus 147

  Ken Christy 151

  Katie Lee 155

The Harold Peary Show 161

  From Summerfield to Melrose Springs 162

    Characters and Cast 167

  Kathryn Card 169

  Jane Morgan 173

  Gloria Holliday 179

  Joseph Kearns 183

  Parley Baer 193

  Olan Soule 197

  Mary Jane Croft 201

  Sammy Ogg 205

Legacy 207

Appendix 215

  Episode Logs 216

    Fibber McGee and Molly 216

    The Great Gildersleeve 221

    The Harold Peary Show 240

  Filmography 242

  Look Who's Laughing (1941) 243
  Here We Go Again (1942) 244
  Seven Days' Leave (1942) 245
  Gildersleeve's Bad Day (1943).. 246
  Gildersleeve on Broadway (1943)... 248
  Gildersleeve's Ghost (1944) 249

 The Television Series 250

  Cast and Characters... 252
  Episode Log 255

 Trivia 257
 Notable Quotes... 261

List of Photos/Illustrations... 262
Works Cited 266
About the Author 275

ii. Actor Harold Peary best known for his role in The Great Gildersleeve. Circa 1945. Public domain.

Introduction

In the 1930s and 1940s, radio witnessed an upsurge of brilliant performers and character actors who captivated audiences with their talents. Many of these individuals had first developed their skills on the vaudeville stage a decade earlier. Radio was a medium that thrived on creativity, enticing its audience with a wide range of narratives and scenarios that ignited their imaginations. In that era, radio reigned supreme as the primary source of entertainment, providing performers and writers alike with countless sought-after opportunities.

Radio programs were incredibly popular, so much so that Hollywood often selected specific personalities from these shows to bring to the big screen. Occasionally, they even adapted the entire program itself, hoping to lure its loyal fans to the theaters. Nevertheless, this distinctive form of entertainment did not consistently translate well onto the silver screen. Radio, in the end, depended on the mental landscapes created by its audience. When faced with Hollywood's interpretation of the stories and the physical appearance of the actors who were previously only voices on the radio, the films often fell short of the expectations fans had formed in their own minds.

A similar phenomenon occurred when television surpassed radio as the primary broadcast medium in the United States during the 1950s. Not all radio programs that made the transition to television were successful.

Since I was a child, I have been utterly enthralled by the mesmerizing craft of storytelling. It stimulated my already active imagination and enabled me to grow as a future writer. In my teens, I found myself drawn to a radio program which rebroadcast old-time radio shows on WNIB in my hometown of Chicago. The program was *Those Were the Days* (1970-2009) hosted by Radio Hall of Fame inductee Chuck Schaden. Every week, I eagerly looked forward to Chuck's curated collection of vintage radio shows and the fascinating guests he brought on.

I had the pleasure of being introduced to timeless classics like *Fibber McGee and Molly, Suspense, The Shadow, The Jack Benny Program, The Bickersons, Inner Sanctum Mysteries, The Phil Harris-Alice Faye Show*, and many other remarkable programs. But one show that truly stood out for me was *The Great Gildersleeve*. In this book, you will discover that the program was one of the first spin-offs in broadcast history. Earlier spin-offs were 1939's *The Right to Happiness* from *The Guiding Light* and *Bright Horizon* from *Big Sister*, which aired a few days before *The Great Gildersleeve's* premier.[1] The program that first introduced the Gildersleeve character to audiences was *Fibber McGee and Molly*.

The Great Gildersleeve captured my attention with its undeniable charm and my profound yearning for the past. When I first stumbled upon old-time radio, I had already developed a strong distaste for the sheer amount of violence, profanity, and disturbing imagery and situations that seemed to pervade films and television. I was yearning for a bit of enchantment and amusement in its purest form. The episodes of *The Great Gildersleeve* revolved around various innocuous themes such as hosting servicemen during Thanksgiving dinner, a visit from a college friend, getting engaged, exploring one's family history, and sponsoring an

---

[1] Cox, Jim. "'Let's All Just Be Jolly Boys!' Well Now, I Wouldn't Say That Mr. Gildersleeve." Old Time Radio Researchers, 2020.

orphan. The entrancing writing and the actors' talent in bringing the diverse characters to life drew me into the story and left me with a feeling of tranquility and joy once I finished listening to each episode. I wanted to share this experience with others and help them explore the world of old-time radio.

And so, I embarked on my first endeavor to write a book. The subject matter was, of course, *The Great Gildersleeve*. In 2000, I participated in my first SPERDVAC convention in Los Angeles, where I encountered numerous individuals who had been professionally involved in the radio industry as well as those who were deeply invested in the hobby. From that point on, I corresponded with various individuals from all over the country who were members or founders of other old-time radio societies and clubs. I connected with these individuals with the intention of expanding my understanding of the golden age of radio and gathering valuable insights for my book. I utilized these resources to acquire every available episode of *The Great Gildersleeve*, whether on tape or CD. I listened to each and every program that was broadcast between 1941 and 1957. The fact that there were a total of 552 episodes broadcast from 1941 to 1954 is quite extraordinary. In the back of this book, you'll find the episode logs for *The Great Gildersleeve, Fibber McGee and Molly*, and *The Harold Peary Show*. The *Fibber McGee and Molly* logs provide a glimpse into the episodes where the Gildersleeve character and others were introduced to fill the void left by Molly's absence. *The Harold Peary Show* was a CBS attempt to recreate the success of *The Great Gildersleeve*.

It's important to note that there are quite a few missing episodes, particularly in the later part of the series. During a time when radio was on the decline, the networks made the decision to reuse the tapes and record over the shows. In some instances, we have knowledge of the title of a particular episode, but regrettably, the recording is not available to the general public.

The renewed fascination with these classic radio broadcasts is truly astounding. Throughout my discussions with Mrs. Waterman, the wife of actor Willard Waterman, her astonishment was obvious as she marveled at the continued appeal of the classic shows and the dedicated community of collectors who cherish these recordings. According to her, Willard viewed it as a mere job and would often discard his script in the trash when he returned home. Consider the immense value that those items hold for collectors in the present day.

Founded in 1966, the Pacific Pioneer Broadcasters (PPB) is committed to safeguarding the rich legacy of West Coast broadcasting during radio's golden age. The golden age began with the birth of commercial radio broadcasting in the early 1920s and lasted through the 1950s, when television gradually replaced radio. Over time, the organization has amassed an impressive collection of radio scripts, memorabilia, and sound recordings that provide a fascinating insight into the rich history of American broadcasting. Unfortunately, the artifacts stored in a bank's basement at Hollywood Boulevard and Vine Street were contaminated by toxic polychlorinated biphenyls due to an underground electrical transformer fire in 2004. They were slated to be included in the American Radio Archives at the Thousand Oaks Library. At that time, the PPB lacked the resources to restore the collection. However, in April 2014, the items were finally donated to the Thousand Oaks Library Foundation, which subsequently conveyed the collection to the University of California in 2021.

Regrettably, no matter how hard I tried, a chain of inevitable circumstances shattered my dreams of getting The Great Gildersleeve manuscript, which I had been diligently crafting, published. I instead decided to embark on a fruitful writing journey, exploring a diverse array of topics. After successfully bringing twelve books to market over the span of eight years, I found myself drawn back to the project that initially sparked my love for writing. I have always maintained a deep and unwavering passion for old-time radio, even in the face of numerous challenges during my formative years as an author. I will reach the pinnacle of my writing career by releasing this book that has been completely revised. I hope it will take you back to a time of innocence and inspire you to rediscover this forgotten medium with a renewed sense of enthusiasm.

iii. Fibber McGee and Molly with Ted Weems and his orchestra broadcasting from Chicago in 1937. Public domain.

Fibber McGee and Molly

iv. Jim and Marian Jordan. Circa 1930s. Public domain.

79 Wistful Vista

A cherished gem of American radio comedy, *Fibber McGee and Molly* left an indelible mark on the world of broadcasting, forever altering its landscape. From its debut in 1935 until its demise in 1959, the program was widely regarded as one of the finest in American popular culture.[2]

During the 1930s and 1940s, very few broadcasters could rival the remarkable success and groundbreaking creativity of Fibber McGee's incredible twenty-four-year radio run. The show played a crucial role in shaping the genre that later became known as situation comedy. Furthermore, the program also spawned two successful spin-off series in the 1940s, featuring the beloved supporting characters Gildersleeve and Beulah.[3]

The origins of *Fibber McGee and Molly* can be traced back to the Jordans' previous radio comedy program, *Smackout*. The program showcased the escapades of Fibber McGee, an innate storyteller (hence the moniker Fibber), and his loyal wife Molly as they navigated life in the lively community of Wistful Vista, surrounded by a colorful group of neighbors and acquaintances. In the 1940s, when the show was at its peak of popularity, RKO Radio Pictures adapted it into a series of feature films. In 1959, there was an endeavor to bring the series to television, featuring a different cast and a team of new writers. Unfortunately, this

---

[2] "Fibber McGee and Molly." Old Radio World, www.oldradioworld.com.
[3] "Fibber McGee and Molly," St. James Encyclopedia of Popular Culture. Encyclopedia.Com. 14 Jun. 2024." Encyclopedia.Com, Encyclopedia.com.

venture turned out to be a critical and commercial failure. The program's end was brought on by Marian Jordan's death shortly thereafter.[4]

The title characters were brought to life by Jim Jordan and Marian Driscoll Jordan, a talented couple who had been collaborating in radio for decades. Both hailing from Peoria, Illinois, they shared a common dream of pursuing music. Jim had dreams of becoming a singer, while Marian had her heart set on becoming a music teacher. The couple were married on August 31, 1918. Five days after the wedding, Jim received his draft notice. He was sent to France and became part of a military touring ensemble that entertained the armed forces. After Jim's return from France, he and Marian made a bold decision to test their luck in the world of vaudeville. Their careers as vaudevillians were rather lackluster, to say the least.

In 1924, Jim and Marian were in Chicago, staying with Jim's brother, when they happened to be listening to the radio. Jim confidently declared that he and Marian could easily outperform the current musical act they were listening to. Jim's brother challenged him to a bet of $10, doubting his ability to accomplish the task. Jim and Marian promptly raced over to station WIBO in order to win the bet. Upon arrival, they were given the opportunity to go on the air. At the end of their performance, the couple was offered a contract for a weekly show. They earned $10 per week. The show's sponsor was Oh Henry! candy, and they appeared for six months on *The Oh Henry! Twins* program before transitioning to radio station WENR in 1927.[5]

---

[4] Fibber McGee and Molly." Wikipedia, Wikimedia Foundation, 29 June 2024.
[5] Fibber McGee and Molly." Wikipedia.

Jim and Marian had hosted or appeared on numerous local music and repartee programs during the early 1930s. Their work gradually developed into a series that ultimately secured them a place on a national NBC hookup.[6]

While working on *The Luke and Mirandy Show* for WENR, Jim Jordan came across an interesting story about a shopkeeper from Missouri. Despite having a store filled with merchandise, the shopkeeper would always claim to be "smack out" of whatever a customer requested, yet he never ran out of tall tales to share.

During their time at WENR, the Jordans had the opportunity to meet Donald (Don) Quinn, a talented cartoonist who was working in radio. Impressed by his skills, the couple decided to bring him on board as their writer in 1931. They collaborated to develop a fifteen-minute daily program for station WMAQ called *Smackout*. The program debuted in 1931, and centered on a general store and its owner, Luke Grey (Jim Jordan). Luke was known for his love of spinning tall tales and his constant inability to have what his customers needed. He always seemed to be "smack out of it." Marian demonstrated her versatility by skillfully portraying multiple characters on the program. She lent her voice to sixty-nine different characters over the course of the show's run. Additionally, she showcased her musical talent by providing piano accompaniment throughout the performance. *Smackout* was acquired by NBC in April 1933 and aired nationally until August 1935. In 1935, *Smackout* gave way to *Fibber McGee and Molly*.[7]

---

[6] Fibber McGee and Molly." Wikipedia.
[7] Fibber McGee and Molly." Wikipedia.

The success of *Smackout* demonstrated the strength of the Jordan-Quinn partnership, but their subsequent creation surpassed all expectations in terms of longevity. Quinn amplified Luke Grey's tendency to exaggerate stories by creating the characters Fibber McGee and Molly. The earlier version of *Fibber McGee and Molly* focused on Fibber's exaggerated stories and drawn-out speeches. In the initial episodes of the series, Molly had a strong Irish dialect, while Fibber's voice was more exaggerated and cartoon-like. As the series progressed into the late 1930s and adopted a more familiar sitcom format, Fibber and Molly switched to more realistic, Americanized dialects that matched their natural tones. The show made its debut on NBC on April 16, 1935. While it took some time for it to gain popularity, it became the highest-rated radio program in the country after three seasons.

The Jordans recognized Quinn's significant contribution and granted him full partnership status. The salary for *Fibber McGee and Molly* was divided between the Jordans and Quinn.

Despite Don's amazing talent, the scripts lacked depth, with each episode revolving around a narrow storyline. The couple seemed to have no visible means of income. Their adventures mostly took place in the McGee home at 79 Wistful Vista, a property they won in a raffle organized by Mr. Hagglemeyer's Wistful Vista Development Company. The McGees moved in on September 2, 1935 and the format that was to establish the show as a leading comedy program began to unfold.

Every week, a colorful cast of supporting characters navigated their way through the house. Even announcer Harlow Wilcox was portrayed as a character, with his role cleverly incorporating a plug for sponsor

Johnson's Wax. Bill Thompson, an extraordinary voice actor, brought to life numerous supporting characters on the show. One of them was Wallace Wimple, a husband who seemed to be in a constant state of torment, his every word dripping with misery. One of the most unforgettable characters was the Old Timer, a cantankerous gabber whose well-known catchphrase, "That ain't the way I heard it!" gained widespread popularity throughout the country in 1940.[8]

Although acknowledged as an early situation comedy, the cast of *Fibber McGee and Molly* had a performance style that resembled more of a vaudeville variety act, incorporating numerous humorous gags. One recurring gag, and perhaps the most famous, involved McGee's closet, a hall closet so overflowing with junk that every time the door was opened, everything would come crashing down in a nearly epic cacophony of sound. Listeners at home could either laugh at the closet of their imaginations or at the sound effects wizardry involved in its creation. Fibber would inevitably say, "I've gotta clean out that closet one of these days" at the end of the final clink.

The jokes generally revolved around Fibber's latest scheme and the reactions of the regular cast of characters, adding a touch of humor to the story. Most of the characters lacked depth, existing only as background figures throughout the entire show. Nevertheless, some characters underwent further development, allowing them to fulfill roles beyond being mere foils for Fibber.[9]

---

[8] "Fibber McGee and Molly," St. James Encyclopedia of Popular Culture.
[9] "The Great Gildersleeve and the Evolution-Revolution of Comedy." Old Time Radio Shows from the Golden Age of Radio, 10 Apr. 2019, www.oldtimeradioshows.com/.

From November 15, 1937 to April 18, 1939, Marian was not able to participate in the show due to a personal struggle with alcoholism. However, the public was informed that her absence was attributed to fatigue. She found herself consumed by her excessive drinking and made the brave decision to seek help at a rehabilitation center in suburban Chicago.[10] During this interim period, the show was renamed *Fibber McGee and Company*, and the scripts ingeniously dealt with Molly's absence.[11]

The show was moved from NBC Chicago to the newly established West Coast Radio City in Hollywood in January 1939.[12] Some people who were familiar with Marian had reservations about her ability to make a comeback in radio. She astonished everyone when she embarked on a solo journey from Joliet, Illinois to Pasadena, California in March 1939. Marian effortlessly slipped back into the role of Molly, impressing listeners who acknowledged that she had improved considerably during her hiatus.[13]

The show continued steadily until 1953, when Marian's health began to deteriorate. She declined her physician's recommendation to take an extended period of rest, opting to continue with her performances. *Fibber McGee and Molly* was then recorded from the Jordans' home in Encino. The program officially ended in 1956, but the Jordans continued their roles as Fibber McGee and Molly in short skits on the NBC radio program *Monitor* until October 2, 1959, when Marian's failing health rendered her unable to continue. *Monitor* attracted audiences across the nation with its

---

[10] "Marian Driscoll Jordan." Wikipedia, Wikimedia Foundation, 29 Apr. 2024.
[11] "Fibber McGee and Molly." Wikipedia.
[12] "Fibber McGee and Molly." Wikipedia.
[13] "Marian Driscoll Jordan." Wikipedia.

live broadcasts on NBC Radio from June 12, 1955 to January 26, 1975. The program aired on weekends, starting at eight a.m. on Saturday and continuing until midnight on Sunday. It featured a captivating mix of broadcasting personalities, including NBC News correspondents, actors, and other well-known figures.

By the time *Fibber McGee and Molly* was adapted for television, Marian was unable to reprise her role due to illness. Cathy Lewis was cast in her place, opposite Bob Sweeney as Fibber. The cancellation of the television series after just half a season was attributed to Lewis' more somber depiction of Molly.

In 1958, Marian received the devastating news that she had an inoperable form of cancer. She passed away peacefully at her home on April 7, 1961.[14]

In 1962, Jim Jordan married Gretchen Stewart, the widow of radio comic Harry Stewart (Yogi Yorgesson). They stayed married for the remainder of his life, and he remained in retirement, with the exception of a brief return to television when he appeared in an episode of *Chico and the Man* (Season 3, Episode 10, aired December 17, 1976).

In March 1988, Jim collapsed at his home and suffered a major stroke. He never regained consciousness and passed away on April 1. He is interred alongside Marian Jordan in the Saint Ann section of Holy Cross Cemetery in Culver City.[15]

---

[14] "Marian Driscoll Jordan." Wikipedia.
[15] "Jim Jordan (Actor)." Wikipedia, Wikimedia Foundation, 30 June 2024.

v. *Writer Don Quinn. Public domain.*

Don Quinn

American comedy writer Don Quinn collaborated with the Jordans on WENR and served as the primary writer for their highly acclaimed radio show *Fibber McGee and Molly* for seventeen years.[16]

Don was born in Grand Rapids, Michigan on November 18, 1900, to parents Jeremiah Francis "Frank" Quinn and Nina Louise Meech.[17] He quit school in the tenth grade to serve in World War I. After the war, Quinn found employment as a freelance cartoonist. It was quite a shock when he discovered that the magazines he sold his cartoons to were keeping his captions but getting rid of his artwork. Don decided to capitalize on his talent for comedy by writing material for the vaudeville duo John Sigvard "Ole" Olsen and Harold Ogden "Chic" Johnson. Before long, he began crafting gags for other comedians too. However, Quinn's writing assignments began to dry up following the 1929 stock market crash.[18]

Quinn packed his bags and moved to Chicago, a city renowned for its thriving radio community, even in the midst of the Great Depression. He landed a position at WENR, where he had the opportunity to write for a talented group of up-and-coming comedians.[19] When he met Jim and Marian Jordan at WENR, Jim Jordan was aware of Quinn's reputation as a comedy writer and requested that he provide material for a program that he and Marian were performing on, *The Farmer Rusk Hour*. Don received

---

[16] Shreve, Ivan G. "Happy Birthday, Don Quinn!" Radio Spirits, 18 Nov. 2018.
[17] FamilySearch.Org, ancestors.familysearch.org.
[18] "Don Quinn." Wikipedia.
[19] Shreve, Ivan G. "Happy Birthday, Don Quinn!"

$10 in compensation for the quips he composed. Later, he was asked to revive *Luke and Mirandy*, an earlier series in which the couple had starred. The new series, *Smackout*, premiered on WMAQ on March 2, 1931. The Jordans received $200 per week for the show, from which they allocated $40 to Don. The trio gained widespread fame when *Smackout* was broadcasted on the NBC network. Before it was discontinued on August 3, 1935, Quinn created a grand total of 948 scripts for the program.

John J. Louis, the head of the advertising firm which served S.C. Johnson & Son, was introduced to *Smackout* by his wife. She spoke highly of the show, suggesting it could be a great sponsorship opportunity for S.C. Johnson. Don received a payment of $75 to come up with a sample script, and the Jordans were cast in the production that later became *The Johnson Wax Program with Fibber McGee and Molly*. The show made its debut on April 16, 1935, on NBC's Red Network.[20]

Unfortunately, Quinn was notorious for prolonging the script-writing process. He was prone to procrastinating until the last minute, at which point he would lock himself in his office with a generous supply of sandwiches, a large kettle of coffee, and two cartons of cigarettes. He would emerge from his office after spending several hours in isolation with a script that was rarely in need of any modifications.[21]

By 1941, the Jordans and Quinn were evenly dividing a paycheck of $6,000 among themselves. In 1943, Don Quinn began to delegate some of his writing responsibilities for *Fibber McGee and Molly* to his

---

[20] Shreve, Ivan G. "Happy Birthday, Don Quinn!"
[21] "Don Quinn." Wikipedia.

apprentice, Phil Leslie, after eight years of serving as the sole writer on the program.

The Jordans sold the rights to *Fibber McGee and Molly* to NBC in order to prevent a "talent raid" from rival CBS, and Quinn was included in the deal. He signed a seven-year exclusive contract with the network and was earning $3,000 per week at the peak of his career for the show.[22]

In 1945, Quinn created *The Beulah Show* for CBS Radio. The program was spun off from *Fibber McGee and Molly* where the character Beulah Brown, served as the McGee's domestic helper. Beulah aired on CBS from 1945 to 1954 and had a television run on ABC from 1950 to 1952.[23] Phil Leslie eventually assumed the role of head writer on the series.[24]

Quinn left the *Fibber McGee and Molly* program at the end of the 1949-50 season in order to pursue other opportunities. In 1950, he created *The Halls of Ivy*, a delightful comedy centered around the president of a small, Midwestern college, and his wife, a former British musical star. The program made its debut on NBC in January 1950 and continued until May 1952. Quinn was the sole writer on the program. Additionally, the program was briefly carried on CBS during the 1954-55 television season. Quinn also made contributions to the television series.[25]

Don officially made his television debut in 1953 as a story editor for *Four-Star Playhouse*. He also contributed to *Climax!, The Dinah Shore*

---

[22] Shreve, Ivan G. "Happy Birthday, Don Quinn!"
[23] "Don Quinn." Wikipedia.
[24] Shreve, Ivan G. "Happy Birthday, Don Quinn!"
[25] "Don Quinn." Wikipedia.

Chevy Show, *The Addams Family*, and provided script consultation for *Petticoat Junction*.

Don Quinn passed away from a heart attack on December 30, 1967, at the age of sixty-seven.[26] He was survived by his second wife Edythe Louise Dixon. Garnette Steve, his first wife, died in 1938 in a fatal car accident. Don and Edythe were married in Chicago on July 7, 1939.[27] Although he had been ill for a considerable period of time, his passing received minimal coverage in the press.[28]

---

[26] "Don Quinn Dead; Top Radio Writer; Creator of 'Fibber McGee and Molly,' a 17-Year Hit." The New York Times, The New York Times, 31 Dec. 1967.
[27] FamilySearch.Org, ancestors.familysearch.org/sl.
[28] "Don Quinn." Wikipedia, Wikimedia Foundation, 29 June 2024..

vi. Jim and Marian Jordan as Fibber McGee and Molly. Fibber's opening the closet and everything falling out was a long-running joke on the radio program. Circa 1948. Public domain.

vii. Throckmorton P. Gildersleeve and Fibber McGee. Circa 1941. Public domain.

Throckmorton P. Gildersleeve

Fibber McGee and Molly was one of the pioneering radio comedies that introduced a cast of recurring characters, played by actors other than the main stars. Nearly all of the characters had recurring phrases and running gags.[29]

One of those recurring characters was Throckmorton P. Gildersleeve. At the outset, the pompous neighbor next door, whom Fibber enjoyed mocking and arguing with, was substantially less three-dimensional. Gildersleeve underwent multiple transformations and name changes before ultimately being given the name Throckmorton.

On April 13, 1936, in an episode titled "Taking Over the Hotel," Don Quinn first unveiled a character named Wallingford Tuttle Gildersleeve. Cliff Arquette was the first actor to portray the character. In the episode titled "The Haircut" that aired on May 4, 1936, Quinn created a character named Clifford Gildersleeve. On September 20, 1938, audiences were introduced to Widdicomb Gildersleeve, a baby carriage manufacturer, in an episode titled "Efficiency Expert in a Baby Carriage Factory." During the airing of the episode "Gildersleeve's Memory Course" on March 14, 1939, actor Harold Peary portrayed the character Cyrus L. Dalrymple, a memory course salesman. On March 21, 1939, we were graced with his familiar voice once more, as he took on the role of Frank the barber in the episode titled "Spring Haircut." On April 25, 1939, Quinn introduced the character Dr. Donald Gildersleeve in the episode "McGee Gets Glasses."

---

[29] Oldtimeradiolovers. "The Great Gildersleeve." Old Time Radio Lovers, 20 Dec. 2019..

Another instance in which Quinn used the name Gildersleeve was on June 20, 1939, when McGee visited Dr. Wilberforce Gildersleeve, a dentist, in the episode titled "Toothache." Eventually, a singular personality began to emerge as these separate characters began to coalesce.[30] Throckmorton P. Gildersleeve made his debut on October 3, 1939, in an episode called "Killer Canova's Autograph."

Peary's voice was perfectly suited for a particular type of characterization that emphasized the depiction of powerful, commanding characters. Quinn believed that because of Fibber McGee's overconfident demeanor, the more pretentious the authority figure, the better.[31] Gildersleeve often responded to Fibber's harsh or critical statements with the catchphrase, "You're a haa-aa-aard man, McGee," adding a touch of humor to their interactions.[32]

In the episode "Raking Leaves," which aired on October 17, 1939, Throckmorton P. Gildersleeve, the proprietor of the Gildersleeve Girdle Works, was already residing in the house next door to the McGees. He displayed a distressingly prickly personality, and because of McGee's own unpredictable and outspoken nature, the two men had no trouble finding subjects to debate as neighbors.[33]

Harold Peary frequently embellished the facts during interviews and asserted that he played a role in assisting Quinn in the development of the character. He claimed the letter "P" in the character's middle name represented Peary, and the name "Throckmorton" was derived from his

---

[30] "Fibber McGee and Molly." Wikipedia, Wikimedia Foundation.
[31] McLeod, Elizabeth. "The Great Gildersleeve: Character Counts." Radio Classics, 31 Aug. 2016.
[32] "Fibber McGee and Molly." Wikipedia.
[33] Cox, Jim. "'Let's All Just Be Jolly Boys!' Well Now, I Wouldn't Say That Mr. Gildersleeve." Old Time Radio Researchers, 2020.

former street address in Chicago. However, after the airing of the "Gildersleeve's Diary" episode on October 22, 1940, it was revealed the character's middle name was "Philharmonic."[34]

Fibber and Molly became immensely popular on radio, leading other sponsors to eagerly seek opportunities to capitalize on their success. Meanwhile, Peary was becoming increasingly irritated and seriously considered quitting the program in 1941, when he got a chance to star in his own show. Despite Johnson's Wax's initial agreement to sponsor the show, they backed out following the May 14, 1941, broadcast of the audition program. The situation appeared bleak until The Kraft Food Company intervened and agreed to sponsor the program. *The Great Gildersleeve* debuted on August 31, 1941, on the NBC Red Network.[35]

NBC officially divided its marketing strategies on January 1, 1927. The "Red Network" provided commercially sponsored entertainment and music programming, while the "Blue Network" primarily disseminated sustaining (non-sponsored) content, particularly news and cultural programs.

The Pacific Coast Network, also known as the NBC Orange Network, was established on April 5, 1927, as part of NBC's expansion to the West Coast. The Pacific Gold Network, also known as the NBC Gold Network, was introduced on October 18, 1931. Programs from the Red Network were broadcast on the Orange Network, while those from the Blue Network were broadcast on the Gold Network. Eventually, the Orange Network affiliate stations were incorporated into the Red Network in

---

[34] Oldtimeradiolovers. "The Great Gildersleeve." Old Time Radio Lovers, 20 Dec. 2019.
[35] "The Great Gildersleeve and the Evolution-Revolution of Comedy." Old Time Radio Shows from the Golden Age of Radio.

1936, and the Gold Network was subsequently incorporated into the Blue Network.[36]

---

[36] "History of NBC." Wikipedia, Wikimedia Foundation, 6 July 2024.

The Great Gildersleeve

viii. Cast of The Great Gildersleeve circa 1948 (Seated from left to right: Lillian Randolph, Gloria Holliday, Una Merkel, and Mary Lee Robb. Standing: Richard LeGrand, Earle Ross, Walter Tetley, Harold Peary, Jack Meakin (Musical director), John Wald (Announcer), and Arthur Q, Bryan. Public domain.

From Wistful Vista to Parkside Avenue

The Great Gildersleeve, a show that set the stage for popular TV series like *Bachelor Father* and *Family Affair*, revolved around a single man who took on the responsibility of caring for his late sister's children. Amidst the challenges of raising children and managing a successful business, he adeptly juggled the responsibilities of his personal and professional life. With time, he came to appreciate his role as Summerfield's water commissioner, loved spending time with women, and looked forward to spending evenings out with his pals. The scripts were skillfully crafted with sophistication and wit, often playfully mocking Gildersleeve's subtly subdued pomposity.[37]

Don Quinn was unable to dedicate the necessary time and effort to write the new series, thus the responsibility was delegated to Leonard L. Levinson, a writer with a style of his own. Levinson possessed a humor that was much more nuanced compared to Quinn's preference for slapstick comedy. It was Levinson's distinctive style that would ultimately shape *The Great Gildersleeve* throughout its entire run. He portrayed Gildersleeve as a compassionate individual beneath his tough exterior. Gildersleeve embraced the responsibility of being a nurturing guardian to his orphaned niece Marjorie and nephew Leroy, showing them unwavering care and support. He treated his maid Birdie with genuine kindness, recognizing her value and treating her with respect. In his adopted town of Summerfield, he remained a steadfast companion to his friends. When Levinson entered the service in 1942, John Whedon

---

[37] "The Great Gildersleeve." ONESMEDIA, www.onesmedia.com.

and Sam Moore took over, propelling *The Great Gildersleeve* to new heights and establishing it as one of the most exceptional character comedies of the 1940s.

The town of Summerfield was meticulously developed by Whedon and Moore, resulting in a vivid and authentic portrayal of small-town America during wartime. A colorful cast of characters would soon gather in Gildersleeve's world. Judge Hooker, Gildersleeve's friend, would be joined by Leila Ransom, his girlfriend, along with Peavey the druggist, Floyd the barber, Police Chief Gates, Bessie the scatterbrained secretary, Mayor Terwilliger, Mr. Bullard, Aunt Hattie, and a host of other individuals, each with their own distinct comedic traits. In this particular context, Throckmorton P. Gildersleeve ("Unky" to Marjorie and "Uncle Mort" to Leroy) gradually emerged as a more authentic, thoughtful, and compassionate individual.[38]

In certain episodes of *Fibber McGee and Molly*, Gildersleeve briefly alluded to his wife, although she never made an appearance on the show. However, in his own series, he was portrayed as a bachelor.

Birdie Lee Coggins, a Black cook and housekeeper, was an indispensable figure in the Gildersleeve household, brought to life with great skill by the talented Lillian Randolph. Throughout the first season, Birdie's character was frequently depicted as lacking intelligence by writer Levinson. Through the passage of time, she experienced a remarkable metamorphosis, evolving into the genuine intellect and nurturer of the

---

[38] McLeod, Elizabeth. "The Great Gildersleeve: Character Counts."

household, all thanks to the profound impact of Whedon and other gifted writers.

During the audition show that aired on May 14, 1941, Gildersleeve's niece Marjorie was originally called Evelyn. Throughout the 1940s, Marjorie's character underwent a transformation, with Lurene Tuttle, Louise Erickson, and Mary Lee Robb all taking on the role at different times. In the ninth season (September 1949-June 1950), a romance blossomed between her and Walter "Bronco" Thompson, a college football player portrayed by Richard Crenna. Their wedding was featured in the May 23, 1950, issue of *Look* magazine. After a few years of residing at the original Forrester residence on 747 Parkside Avenue, the couple welcomed twins and decided to move into the house next door.

In the spring of 1949, Leroy, Gildersleeve's nephew (played by Walter Tetley), began to mature after spending the majority of the 1940s as a young boy between the ages of ten and twelve. He developed strong bonds with the girls living in the Bullard household just across the street. He cultivated a profound passion for driving, embraced the art of playing the drums, and nurtured dreams of pursuing a musical career.

In the vast array of individuals that filled his life, Gildersleeve (Gildy) had a unique connection with Judge Horace Hooker (portrayed by Earle Ross), who held the significant responsibility of overseeing his brother-in-law's estate. However, their partnership was marked by numerous conflicts during the early broadcasts. Following a shift in scriptwriters in January 1943, the conflicts gradually diminished and the two men forged an enduring friendship.

In the second season, pharmacist Richard Q. Peavey, played by Richard LeGrand, and barber Floyd Munson, initially portrayed by Mel Blanc and later by Arthur Q. Bryan, became part of Gildersleeve's social circle. In the fourth season, a group of friends, under the guidance of Police Chief Donald Gates (played by Ken Christy), formed the Jolly Boys Club. Immersed in the world of barbershop quartet singing, they honed their skills while sipping bottles of Coca-Cola.

Gildersleeve had numerous encounters with different women throughout the series, and even came close to getting married three times before deciding to take a more relaxed approach to dating.

In 1950, Harold Peary was persuaded to move *The Great Gildersleeve* to CBS. However, the sponsor Kraft refused to support the decision. Peary's contractual obligations with CBS prevented him from appearing as a star performer on NBC. Consequently, Willard Waterman was selected as Peary's replacement.[39]

Waterman and Peary had a strong bond that developed during their time together on Chicago radio. Interestingly, Waterman took over the role of the sheriff in *The Tom Mix Ralston Straightshooters* program after Peary's departure in the 1930s. His voice closely resembled Peary's, although he chose not to imitate Peary's distinctive laugh as the Great Gildersleeve. Peary allegedly filed a lawsuit in an attempt to keep the rights to both the Gildersleeve character and his vocalizations. Waterman sided with Peary on the belief that only one person could claim ownership of the Gildersleeve laugh.[40]

---

[39] Oldtimeradiolovers. "The Great Gildersleeve."
[40] "The Great Gildersleeve." ONESMEDIA.

In mid-1952, a number of the program's familiar characters, including Judge Hooker, Floyd Munson, Marjorie, and her husband Bronco, were noticeably absent for long stretches of time. Joining the program were a pair of fresh faces - Mr. Cooley, the egg man, and Mrs. Potter, the hypochondriac.

In 1953, Gildersleeve's romantic relationships became the main focus of the show. His numerous love interests were constantly changing, and women came and went frequently. Meanwhile, his adversary shifted from Mr. Bullard to Dr. Clarence Olsen portrayed by George N. Neise. [41]

The Great Gildersleeve was not initially part of the fall schedule in the 1954–1955 season, but it made a comeback in November with fifteen-minute episodes airing five times a week. Gildersleeve, Leroy, and Birdie were the only ones who stayed on as regulars on the show. With budget cuts, the other characters rarely made an appearance, and Marjorie and her family, along with the studio audience, and live orchestra were eliminated. The series finally ended its run in 1958.[42]

The program, along with many other radio series, was adversely affected by the emergence of television. In 1955, NBC produced and syndicated a televised version of the series that also featured Waterman. However, the series only lasted thirty-nine episodes. The fifteen-minute radio program and the television show were both produced concurrently during that year.

In the television series, Gildersleeve was portrayed as a character with a more overt womanizing nature, a pompous demeanor, and a slightly less endearing personality. Harold Peary noted that the television series

---
[41] "The Great Gildersleeve." ONESMEDIA.
[42] Oldtimeradiolovers. "The Great Gildersleeve."

encountered similar obstacles as other radio programs when making the leap to the visual medium. In the end, it fell short of what the audience had hoped for. Peary stated that "Waterman was a very tall man" and "Gildersleeve was not a tall man; he was a little man who thought he was a tall man." Peary concluded that, "Willard [Waterman] did a very good job on the radio show" despite being "miscast on the television version."[43]

---

[43] "The Great Gildersleeve." Wikipedia, Wikimedia Foundation, 4 June 2024.

Characters and Cast

Throckmorton P. Gildersleeve
Harold Peary (1941-1950)
Willard Waterman (1950-1958)

Leroy Forrester (nephew)
Walter Tetley

Marjorie Forrester (niece)
Lurene Tuttle (1941-1944)
Louise Erickson (1944-1948)
Mary Lee Robb (1948-1954)

Birdie Lee Coggins (housekeeper)
Lillian Randolph
(Sister Amanda Randolph filled in during the 4/16/57 episode)

Judge Horace Hooker
Earle Ross

Richard Q. Peavey (pharmacist)
Richard LeGrand, Forrest Lewis

Walter "Bronco" Thompson
Richard Crenna

Bronco's parents
Jeanette Nolan
Joe Forte, Joseph Kearns

Ben Waterford
Ben Alexander

Floyd Munson (barber)
Mel Blanc, Arthur Q. Bryan

Donald Gates (police chief)
Ken Christy

Rumson Bullard (neighbor)
Gale Gordon, Jim Backus

Piggy Banks
Tommy Cook

Bessie (Gildersleeve's secretary)
Pauline Drake, Gloria Holiday

Dr. Clarence Olsen
George N. Neise

Mayor Silas B. Terwilliger
Stan Ferrar

Gildersleeve's girlfriends

Leila Ranson
Shirley Mitchell

Adaline Fairchild
Una Merkel

Eve Goodwin
Bea Benaderet

Ellen Bullard Knickerbocker
Martha Scott

Nurse Katherine Milford
Principal Irene Henshaw
Cathy Lewis
(Principal Irene Henshaw was also played by Barbara Eiler)

Grace Tuttle
Mary Shipp

Marie Olsen
Gladys Holland

Joanne Piper
Janet Waldo

Leonard Levinson

American radio writer and author Leonard Louis Levinson was born on March 2, 1904, in Pittsburgh, Pennsylvania. Throughout his time at Fifth Avenue High School in Pittsburgh, he showcased remarkable talents in both athletics and academics. Aside from his impressive athletic accomplishments, he also took on leadership roles in the literary and debate clubs, as well as overseeing the business operations of the school paper. Following his graduation, he set out to study radio engineering at Carnegie Institute of Technology. Afterwards, he made the choice to delve deeper into his passion for drama by enrolling at the University of Pittsburgh. He subsequently continued his studies at the University of California, Los Angeles. During his time, Levinson found employment at a local newspaper.

In 1939, Levinson embarked on a new career in the radio industry. *Joe Penner's Tip Top Show* was among the first shows to use his scripts. He began working with Don Quinn as an assistant writer on *Fibber McGee and Molly* in 1940. He subsequently started writing for *The Great Gildersleeve* in 1941. He resigned from that position in 1942 to become a member of the United States Office of War Information. He had been engaged in pro-democracy radio propaganda in Hollywood for an extended period, as reported by the trade magazine *Variety*. He had attempted to obtain approval from the federal government to address concerns from sponsors about making jokes about the Axis Powers but was unsuccessful. He went on to write for various radio programs after his time with the government, making contributions to popular shows like

The Al Jolson-Monty Woolley Show, *Hollywood Showcase*, *Theater of the Air*, *The Jack Carson Show*, *The Stu Erwin Show*, and *Family Theatre*. Later on, Levinson ventured into the realm of television, lending his talents to projects like *Success Story* and *Sure as Fate*.[44]

In addition to his radio and television work, Levinson wrote the book for the 1945 musical *Mr. Strauss Goes to Boston*, and in the late 1940s served as the chief executive of Impossible Pictures, a producer of animated cartoons.

Regrettably, Leonard Levinson passed away in Los Angeles on January 30, 1974. He was sixty-nine years old.[45]

---

[44] "Leonard Levinson." Wikipedia, Wikimedia Foundation, 19 Apr. 2024.
[45] "Leonard Levinson, Radio Writer, Dies." The New York Times, The New York Times, 2 Feb. 1974, www.nytimes.com.

ix. Advertisement for The Great Gildersleeve presented by Kraft. Compliments of Kraft Foods, Inc.

x. Harold Peary as the star of The Great Gildersleeve, circa 1940s. Photo by Ernest Bachrach. Public domain.

Harold Peary

Harold (Hal) Peary was a renowned American actor, comedian, and singer who worked in radio, film, and television. He is most notably recognized for his role as Throckmorton P. Gildersleeve, a supporting character on *Fibber McGee & Molly* that transitioned into his own radio hit show, *The Great Gildersleeve*.[46]

Jose Pereira de Faria, Peary's birth name, was born on July 25, 1908, to Maude Focha and José (Joseph) P. Faria. Joe Faria was born in Portugal, while his wife Maude was born in California to Portuguese immigrant parents.[47] From an early age, Hal cultivated a fervent interest in music and by 1919, he was showcasing his talent as a young boy soprano at weddings, banquets, and other community gatherings near his parents' residence in San Leandro, California.[48] He made his radio debut as *The Oakland Tribune's Boy Caruso* two years later, and his voice was frequently heard on several Bay Area radio stations during the 1920s and early 1930s. In 1928, he made an appearance on *The Spanish Serenader*, a program aired by a San Francisco NBC affiliate. Later, he took on roles for NBC's *One Man's Family* before moving to Chicago in 1935. Peary became a member of the stock company for the horror program *Lights Out* in Chicago and also had brief stints on *Kaltenmeyer's Kindergarten*, *Welcome Valley*, and *Flying Time*.[49] He demonstrated his flexibility as an actor during this time by playing up to

---

[46] "Harold Peary." Hollywood Walk of Fame, 9 Dec. 2020, walkoffame.com.
[47] Williams, C.S. "Harold Peary: The Great Gildersleeve and More." Classic Film Aficionados, 24 Jan. 2017.
[48] Hastings, Deborah. "Harold Peary, Star of Radio's 'great Gildersleeve,' 76, Dies." Los Angeles Times, Los Angeles Times, 1 Apr. 1985, www.latimes.com.
[49] Shreve, Ivan G. "Happy Birthday, Harold Peary!" Radio Spirits, 25 July 2003.

six different characters in a single radio broadcast, showcasing both his comedic and dramatic skills.[50] According to an article published in *Radio Life* magazine, Peary was casually referred to as "the man who carries colored pencils." Having to play several parts in a single episode, he devised a plan to keep up with himself by color-coding each role on the script.

On September 20, 1938, Peary made an appearance on the *Fibber McGee and Molly* program, portraying a character named Widdicomb P. Gildersleeve. He was the president of a baby carriage manufacturing company.[51] When the *Fibber McGee and Molly* program relocated to the West Coast, Peary followed. He emerged as Fibber McGee's nemesis and neighboring rival, Throckmorton P. Gildersleeve.[52] During the years 1939 to 1941, Gildersleeve took on the role of the only resident of Wistful Vista who possessed enough arrogance to rival McGee. The character achieved significant success and even made an appearance in the film "Look Who's Laughing" in 1941, alongside the McGees.

Despite his other radio appearances, such as his brief stint as Herb Woodley on *Blondie*, Peary began to feel restless in his role as Gildersleeve. He worried about being type-cast and was frustrated that his musical abilities were not being utilized. He gave serious thought to leaving the program, but both NBC and *Fibber McGee and Molly's* sponsor, Johnson's Wax, were eager to keep him on board. They convinced the actor-singer to consider a "spin-off" program called *The*

---

[50] Hastings, Deborah. "Harold Peary, Star of Radio's 'great Gildersleeve,' 76, Dies.".
[51] Stumpf, Charles, and Ben Ohmart. "The Great Gildersleeve."
[52] Shreve, Ivan G. "Happy Birthday, Harold Peary!"

Great Gildersleeve. The first episode was broadcasted on NBC on August 31, 1941.[53]

Gildersleeve was transplanted from Wistful Vista to Summerfield, undergoing not just a change in location but also a transformation in his personal life. Now a bachelor, he'd become less pompous and cantankerous. Additionally, he had taken on the role of caretaker for his orphaned niece and nephew and became more domesticated.[54] He also had the responsibility of managing his late brother-in-law's estate. One aspect of the estate, and his initial duty, was Quig's Open All Night Drug Store. It soon became clear that the store was not doing well. Gildersleeve's bookkeeper described one month's business as, "Much better. We only lost $213.00."[55] Gildersleeve himself was filled with worry. He exclaimed, "It's such a headache it'll soon start to break even just on the aspirin I buy there. I never wanted to operate that cut-rate medicine market in the first place."[56]

The Forrester estate came into possession of the drug store due to an interesting turn of events. It all began when the pharmacist, instead of focusing on his practice, decided to embark on the peculiar endeavor of training a cat. As Gildersleeve put it, "The cat got so good and business got so bad he took the cat to Hollywood and we got the business for the rent."[57] Business was so bad that Judge Hooker urged Gildersleeve to sell the pharmacy, which he eventually did to the City Drug Chain.[58] As for

---

[53] Shreve, Ivan G. "Happy Birthday, Harold Peary!"
[54] "Harold Peary." Hollywood Walk of Fame.
[55] Smith, Mickey C. "Images of Pharmacy and Pharmacists in Old-Time Radio: A Profile of Richard Q. Peavey." JSTOR, Pharmacy in History, 1983, www.jstor.org.
[56] Smith, Mickey C. "Images of Pharmacy and Pharmacists in Old-Time Radio: A Profile of Richard Q. Peavey."
[57] Smith, Mickey C.
[58] Smith, Mickey C.

his own endeavors, Gildersleeve refocused his efforts on his new role as water commissioner of Summerfield after winding down his girdle manufacturing business in Wistful Vista.[59]

During the peak of the show's success, Harold Peary, fully embracing his Gildersleeve persona, lent his voice to three albums for Capitol Records. These albums showcased his ability to captivate young audiences through his engaging readings of beloved children's stories. Released in 1945, *Stories for Children, Told in His Own Way by the Great Gildersleeve* marked Capitol's first ever release for children. The performance included "Puss in Boots," "Rumpelstiltskin," and "Jack and the Beanstalk," accompanied by an orchestra. The second album, *Children's Stories as Told by the Great Gildersleeve,* was released in 1946 and included "Hansel and Gretel" and "The Brave Little Tailor." The third and last album in the series, which was released in 1947, featured the stories "Snow White and Rose Red" and "Cinderella." The music for all three albums was composed by Robert Emmett Dolan. The stories were skillfully adapted to Gildersleeve's distinct demeanor by *The Great Gildersleeve*'s principal writers, Sam Moore and John Whedon.[60]

The Great Gildersleeve kept Peary busy with radio work, but he also appeared on various other programs such as *The Abbott & Costello Show, Calling All Cars, The CBS Radio Workshop, Command Performance, Duffy's Tavern, The Edgar Bergen & Charlie McCarthy Show, Everyman's Theatre, Family Theatre, The First Nighter Program, Guest Star, Hail and Farewell, Hollywood Star Time, The Kraft Music Hall, The Lady Esther/Camel Screen Guild Theatre, The Lux Radio Theatre, Mail Call, The Railroad Hour, The*

---

[59] "Harold Peary." Hollywood Walk of Fame.
[60] "The Great Gildersleeve." ONESMEDIA.

Rudy Vallee Sealtest/Philip Morris Show, *The Sealtest Variety Theatre*, *The Signal Carnival*, *The Sinclair Wiener Minstrels*, *Stars Over Hollywood*, and *The Tony Martin Show*.[61]

One of Peary's worst professional mistakes was deciding to transfer to CBS amid the talent raids. He was convinced that he could bring *The Great Gildersleeve* along with him, but unfortunately, Kraft Foods, the show's sponsor, refused to give their approval. Harold made an effort to create a similar program on CBS, known as *The Harold Peary Show*, but unfortunately, it only lasted one season.[62]

Like other radio actors of the day, Peary made the switch to television, making appearances as a guest star on a number of programs, including *Private Secretary*, *Surfside 6*, *The Dick Van Dyke Show*, *My Mother the Car*, *Petticoat Junction*, *That Girl*, *The Doris Day Show,* and *The Brady Bunch*.[63] He also played the part of Perry Bannister on June Havoc's 1954-55 sitcom *Willy*, and reprised his Herb Woodley role in the first of two video incarnations of *Blondie* after the show transitioned to television in 1957. Peary wasn't asked to play the Great Gildersleeve when the character made his television debut, but he did wind up portraying Mayor La Trivia when the disastrous decision to bring *Fibber McGee and Molly* to television without the Jordans came about in 1959.[64]

Harold Peary's distinctive voice was later featured in animated films by renowned companies such as Hanna-Barbera (*The Galloping Ghost*) and Rankin-Bass (*Rudolph's Shiny New Year*). He also made a number of

---

[61] Shreve, Ivan G. "Happy Birthday, Harold Peary!"
[62] Shreve, Ivan G. "Happy Birthday, Harold Peary!"
[63] Peary, 'Great Gildersleeve,' Dies at 76, The Milwaukee Journal, 1 Apr. 1985.
[64] Shreve, Ivan G. "Happy Birthday, Harold Peary!"

movies based on Gildersleeve's character and others including *Comin' Round the Mountain, Look Who's Laughing, Country Fair, Here We Go Again, Seven Days' Leave, The Great Gildersleeve, Gildersleeve's Bad Day, Gildersleeve on Broadway, Gildersleeve's Ghost,* and *Clambake*.[65]

Peary passed away on March 30, 1985, at the age of seventy-six in Torrance, California, following a heart attack. He had been married on three separate occasions.[66] On May 14, 1929, Harold married dancer Eleanor Virginia (Betty) Jourdaine. The couple met in a California children's theatrical company while they were both in grammar school, according to an article published in *The Capital Times* on August 31, 1941.[67] In February 1946, Harold and Betty shared their decision to part ways, marking the end of a marriage that had endured for almost seventeen years. During the last days of April, news broke out about the divorce proceedings, and eventually, a settlement was reached regarding the property. Just when it seemed like the divorce was about to be finalized in a matter of weeks, Peary dropped a bombshell by revealing his engagement to Gloria Holliday, a fellow member of his radio program. At the time, Betty was living in Nevada. In mid-May, she made her way back to Los Angeles and took legal action, claiming mental cruelty. The divorce was officially finalized on June 20, 1947.[68]

Peary's second wife, Gloria Holliday, was sixteen years his junior. She was a singer and actress, known for her role as Bessie on *The Great Gildersleeve*. Harold and Gloria were unofficially married in a private

---

[65] Peary, 'Great Gildersleeve,' Dies at 76, The Milwaukee Journal, 1 Apr. 1985.
[66] Hastings, Deborah. "Harold Peary, Star of Radio's 'great Gildersleeve,' 76, Dies.".
[67] "'The Great Gildersleeve' on WIBA Today at 4:40." Newspapers.Com, The Capital Times, 31 Aug. 1941.
[68] "Harold Peary: The Great Gildersleeve and More." Classic Film Aficionados, 24 Jan. 2017.

ceremony on July 8, 1946, in Tijuana, Mexico. On March 9, 1947, the Peary family welcomed their son, Harold Jose Faria, who later changed his name to Page Peary. The couple formally tied the knot on June 24, 1947, just four days after the dissolution of Peary's first marriage to Betty Jourdaine. Holliday and Peary ended their marriage amicably in the spring of 1956.[69]

Harold married Callie Juanita Parker, an electrical engineer, on Valentine's Day in 1964. Parker and Peary were both residents of Manhattan Beach, California at the time. Peary was thirteen years older than Parker, and the couple remained married until Callie's passing in a convalescent home in Manhattan Beach on December 11, 1977, after a long illness.[70]

According to his son, Page, the veteran actor retired in 1981 after nearly seventy years in show business. A longtime resident of Manhattan Beach, he was named honorary mayor of the city in 1956.[71]

---

[69] "Harold Peary: The Great Gildersleeve and More."
[70] "Harold Peary: The Great Gildersleeve and More."
[71] Hastings, Deborah. "Harold Peary, Star of Radio's 'great Gildersleeve,' 76, Dies.".

xi. Harold and his first wife, Betty. Public domain.

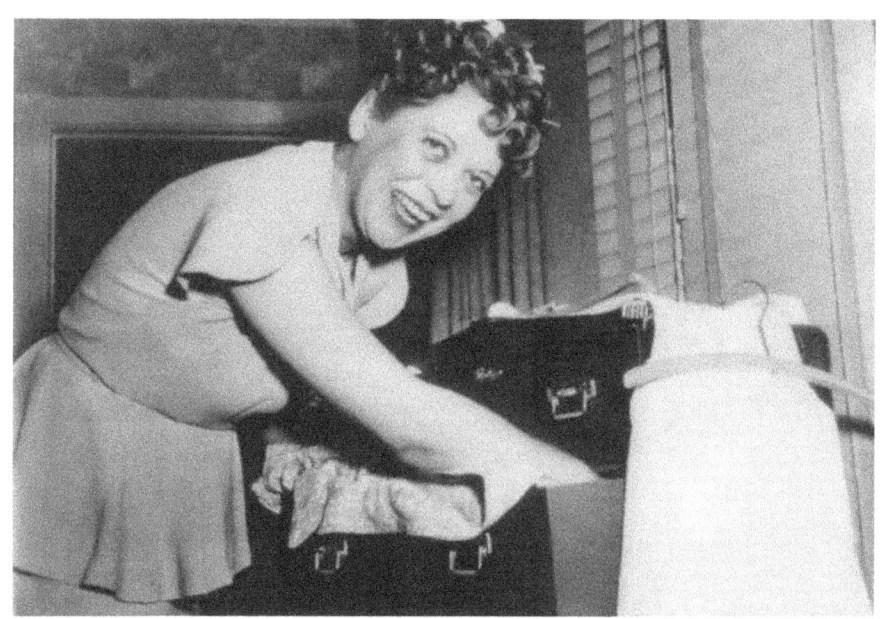

xii. 1946 press photo of Betty Peary, the wife of actor Harold Peary, Beverly Hills. Public domain.

xiii. Publicity photo featuring Harold Peary, his wife Gloria, and their son Page Peary. Circa late 1940s. Public domain.

xiv. Harold Peary and his son Page at Kiddieland. Circa 1952. Public domain.

xv. Willard Waterman as Mr. Merriweather in the U.S. television situation comedy The Halls of Ivy. Circa 1950. Public domain.

xvi. Willard Waterman and Shirley Mitchell. Circa 1956. Public domain.

Willard Waterman

Willard Lewis Waterman, born on August 29, 1914, in Madison, Wisconsin, would forgo his engineering studies at the University of Wisconsin to become a well-known actor in radio, television, stage, and film. A veritable jack of all trades on the radio, he appeared in a variety of roles on programs such as *Chicago Theater of the Air*, *The Tom Mix Ralston Straight Shooters*, *The Halls of Ivy*, *Those Websters*, *The Guiding Light*, and *Lonely Women* from the mid-1930s to the 1950s. Additionally, Waterman starred in a number of films, including *The Apartment*, *Three Coins in the Fountain*, and *Riding High*. His film success opened the door for him to showcase his talents on stage. In 1958, he portrayed the character Claude Upson in the film *Auntie Mame*. In 1966, he had the honor of being chosen to portray Dwight Babcock in the musical *Mame*. In 1973, he embarked on a new adventure by becoming a part of the cast of *The Pajama Game*. This was just the beginning of his journey, as he went on to showcase his talents in the national companies of *A Funny Thing Happened on the Way to the Forum* and *How to Succeed in Business Without Really Trying*. However, Waterman is perhaps best known for his portrayal of the main character in *The Great Gildersleeve*, taking over the role from Harold Peary at the height of the show's popularity.[72]

Waterman developed a passion for show business from a tender age. During his time at Central High School, he became a member of a quartet

---

[72] "Willard Waterman." Wikipedia, Wikimedia Foundation, 6 June 2024.

that entertained listeners with musical interludes during program breaks on Madison's WIBA radio station.[73]

Midway through the 1930s, while he was a student at the University of Wisconsin, Willard worked as a student announcer at WHA, the university's radio station. In addition, he took part in various student performances.[74] The numerous extracurricular activities he was engaged in proved to be a distraction from his engineering studies, ultimately resulting in his expulsion. He relocated to Chicago, a well-known broadcasting hub during that era, and began his career at NBC.[75] His first role was as a villain in the radio series *Chandu the Magician*. Unfortunately, his character met an untimely demise in the first episode. Afterwards, Waterman was cast in *The Tom Mix Ralston Straight Shooters* program in a succession of brief roles that ultimately culminated in the character's demise.[76] Willard did play the part of Tom Mix for one week but was replaced soon after. He was told that he was not dominating the show as he should. The fact of the matter was that Willard who was six foot three inches tall was sharing the microphone with the diminutive Jane Webb. It would have been difficult for any actor to dominate the show under those circumstances.

The Tom Mix Ralston Straight Shooters program, based on Hollywood's original cowboy star, made its debut in New York on September 25, 1933. After the program moved to Chicago, Jack Holden became the new voice of Tom Mix, replacing Artells "Art" Dickson. Waterman and Peary were then brought in to play supporting roles. Waterman, who had a strong

---

[73] Gilliland, Norman. "The Great Willard Waterman." Wisconsin Life, 10 Feb. 2018.
[74] Gilliland, Norman. "The Great Willard Waterman."
[75] Gilliland, Norman. "The Great Willard Waterman."
[76] Shreve, Ivan G. "Happy Birthday, Willard Waterman!" Radio Classics, 29 Aug. 2016.

physical resemblance to Peary and a voice that closely matched his, formed a long-lasting friendship with the man he would eventually replace in *The Great Gildersleeve*.[77]

After establishing himself as a prominent figure in the Chicago radio scene, Willard made the move to Los Angeles, where he continued to shine as a radio star. He moved to Hollywood after the production of a show he was involved in, *Those Websters*, relocated there.[78] Waterman's schedule became exceedingly hectic shortly thereafter, with an average of forty performances per week. His workdays were exceedingly long, beginning at seven in the morning and ending at ten at night. In those days, his voice could be heard across three separate networks for at least forty-five minutes every day.[79] During the mid-thirties the typical soap opera paid a supporting actor anywhere from $2.50 - $5.00. One can see why Willard had to keep busy.

Waterman began appearing on *The Great Gildersleeve* program in 1947, primarily in supporting roles. On May 8, 1947, he was heard as a doctor giving Gildersleeve an insurance exam. On December 24, he returned as Santa Claus.[80]

In 1950, after Peary transitioned to CBS, Waterman was brought in to portray the blundering yet lovable Throckmorton P. Gildersleeve.[81] Playing this role was quite a challenge as the character's success relied heavily on capturing Peary's unique intonation and laughter. Waterman's entire career was at stake, as he had to ensure that he could captivate the

---

[77] "Willard Waterman." Wikipedia.
[78] "Willard Waterman Collection." Old Time Radio, www.otrcat.com.
[79] Gilliland, Norman. "The Great Willard Waterman."
[80] Stumpf, Charles, and Ben Ohmart. "The Great Gildersleeve."
[81] Gilliland, Norman. "The Great Willard Waterman."

audience throughout. In the first episode of the season, the writers dared to draw attention to the cast change instead of brushing it aside.[82]

In Willard's first episode, "Marjorie Is Pregnant," which aired on September 6, 1950, the Gildersleeve family excitedly awaits the great man's return from a long vacation. Shortly after, Gildersleeve makes his big entrance through the front door, proclaiming, "Birdie, I'm home!" Birdie says, "Why you sure look fine, Mr. Gildersleeve," and Throckmorton responds, "I'm a new man, Birdie!" When Leroy, his nephew, enquires about his whereabouts, "Uncle Mort" nonchalantly replies that he spent time at Española Hot Springs, indulging in invigorating sulfur waters and rejuvenating mud baths. Leroy quickly responds, "That must have been high powered mud, you even look different!" The comment provokes a lively reaction from the studio audience, with their laughter resonating in the background.

Although Waterman's voice resembled Peary's, he opted not to betray him by imitating his unique laugh and other mannerisms. Instead, he came up with his own chortle which he referred to as "the Gildersleeve social chuckle." With his own technique and all of the sounds which distinguished the character written into the script, he captivated the audience, the cast, and the reviewers by the end of that first show.[83] Waterman played the lead role on radio from 1950 to 1957, as well as in a short-lived television series that aired in 1955.[84]

When the show made the transition to television, Willard was quite pleased because he felt that it gave him a shot in the arm. By this time, he

---

[82] "Willard Waterman." Wikipedia.
[83] Gilliland, Norman. "The Great Willard Waterman."
[84] "Willard Waterman." Wikipedia.

felt that he was stagnating as an actor and needed something to stir him up. The program provided the right amount of challenge and proved to be just what Willard needed.

By 1973, Waterman had mostly retired from acting. However, in 1980, he made a special appearance in the "Boss and Peterson" radio commercial for Sony. This specific commercial garnered him a highly esteemed Clio Award, an annual accolade bestowed to honor ingenuity and artistic excellence in the realm of advertising.

Like Harold Peary, Willard Waterman also held honorary titles such as the Honorary Water Commissioner of both San Francisco, California and Boise, Idaho. Willard was also given the title of Admiral in the Confederate Navy.

Waterman was a founding member of the American Federation of Radio Artists, the first labor union in radio, in 1937. This organization subsequently evolved into the American Federation of Television and Radio Artists.[85]

On February 2, 1995, Willard Waterman peacefully passed away in his home in Burlingame, California, after battling a bone marrow disease. He was laid to rest at Skylawn Memorial Park in San Mateo, California.[86] His wife, Mary Anna to whom he had been married to for fifty-eight years, passed away on January 15, 2004. The couple had two daughters, Lynne Waterman Ansara and Susan Waterman.

---

[85] "Actor Willard Waterman Dead at 80 - UPI Archives." UPI, UPI, 3 Feb. 1995.
[86] "Willard Waterman." Wikipedia.

xvii. Walter Tetley circa 1940. Public domain.

Walter Tetley

Walter Tetley, born on June 2, 1915, as Walter Campbell Tetzlaff, was an American actor renowned for his exceptional portrayal of child characters on radio from the early 1930s to the mid-1950s. He depicted Leroy Forrester on *The Great Gildersleeve* and Julius Abbruzio on *The Phil Harris-Alice Faye Show*. In addition, he lent his voice to various animated cartoons, advertisements, and spoken-word record albums. He is widely acclaimed for his portrayal of Sherman in the beloved Jay Ward-Bill Scott television series, *Peabody's Improbable History*.[87]

In the 1920s, Tetley's career took off as he expertly channeled the famous Scottish comedian, Harry Lauder. With his unique Scottish and German heritage, Tetley had a natural grasp of the Scottish dialect. Lauder played a significant role in boosting Tetley's career by publicly endorsing him and allowing him to be promoted as "Wee Harry Lauder." As the 1930s rolled in, Tetley became a favorite among radio audiences with his entertaining Scottish routine. He made appearances on various programs, including the 1931 children's serials *The Lady Next Door*, *Let's Pretend*, and the long-running *NBC Children's Hour*, later renamed *Coast-to-Coast on a Bus*. Tetley was a regular guest on this show for a considerable part of the decade. In 1934, he took a break from radio to tour England. During this time, he mesmerized crowds in music halls with his highly praised Lauder performances.[88]

---

[87] "Walter Tetley." Wikipedia, Wikimedia Foundation, 11 June 2024.
[88] McLeod, Elizabeth. "Eternal Youth: Walter Tetley, Radio's Essential Kid." RadioSpirits.Com - Walter Tetley, 2012.

xviii. Walter Tetley performing his Scottish routine. Public domain.

Upon returning to the United States, the nineteen-year-old worked with a number of prominent radio personalities, including Bob Hope, Eddie Cantor, W.C. Fields, Joe Penner, Jim and Marian Jordan, Jack Benny, George Burns and Gracie Allen, Bob Burns, Dinah Shore, Orson Welles, Alan Young, and Jack Paar.[89] However, in the midst of all this success, Walter began experiencing something quite out of the ordinary. When he reached the age of twenty, his physical appearance and voice continued to bear a striking resemblance to that of a twelve-year-old boy. As time passed, speculative gossip and rumors began to circulate about him. Bill Scott, his co-star, playfully insinuated that Tetley had undergone castration. It is possible that Tetley may have been affected by Kallmann syndrome.[90] Kallmann syndrome (KS) is a genetic disorder that interrupts the natural course of puberty in those who are affected. Typically, diagnosis occurs during adolescence when puberty does not begin. It is more frequently observed in males than in females.[91]

The Tetley family never offered a formal explanation for Walter's condition. His career took a significant hit, and he experienced a profound sense of loneliness in his personal life. His condition created a constant feeling of not belonging among his radio colleagues, making it challenging for him to feel comfortable around them. He preferred to spend the majority of his leisure time in seclusion. Rarely did he permit anyone to visit his home.[92]

In 1937, Tetley and his mother made the decision to move to California, where they hoped to find new opportunities. The talented actor swiftly

---

[89] Shreve, Ivan G. "Happy Birthday, Walter Tetley!" Radio Classics, 2 June 2018.
[90] McLeod, Elizabeth. "Eternal Youth: Walter Tetley, Radio's Essential Kid."
[91] "Kallmann Syndrome." Wikipedia, Wikimedia Foundation, 29 May 2024.
[92] McLeod, Elizabeth. "Eternal Youth: Walter Tetley, Radio's Essential Kid."

secured supporting roles in several movies. Unfortunately, Walter found himself stuck in a never-ending cycle of mundane roles such as messengers, bellhops, elevator operators, and office assistants. Now in his twenties, Walter's facial features underwent a subtle transformation, yet his body and voice were still that of a young boy. Tetley's potential for a more significant movie career was hampered by this visually unsettling combination.[93]

Luckily, Tetley had made it to Hollywood just in the nick of time to witness the flourishing radio industry in the heart of the film capital. In the late thirties, a wave of major programs began moving to the west, opening up numerous job opportunities for Walter.

Directors quickly discovered that working with child actors was a challenging task, filled with unexpected surprises, inconsistency, and frustration. Walter Tetley was a seasoned professional, known for his unwavering reliability and ability to stay focused during rehearsals. He never missed a cue and always delivered his lines flawlessly.[94]

In 1941, Walter Tetley found himself in a role that would secure his place in the annals of old-time radio history. Harold Peary was granted a spin-off with *The Great Gildersleeve*. In the program, Gildersleeve's nephew Leroy was quite the mischievous character, endearing himself to radio listeners. In the opening episode, a misguided Leroy insists that his uncle is the manager at the "Gildersleeve Girder-works," an entirely different type of foundation work! This misconception prompted what was to become one of Gildersleeve's famous remarks to his nephew, "You're a

---

[93] McLeod, Elizabeth. "Eternal Youth: Walter Tetley, Radio's Essential Kid."
[94] McLeod, Elizabeth. "Eternal Youth: Walter Tetley, Radio's Essential Kid."

bri-i-i-ght boy, Leroy!" Leroy served as the perfect remedy for Gildersleeve's inflated ego. He often exclaimed, "What a character!" in response to his uncle's pomposity. Despite occasionally causing his uncle some trouble, Leroy had a genuine fondness for him, affectionately referring to him as "Unk." Tetley portrayed the character of Leroy until the show concluded its impressive seventeen-year run on March 27, 1958.[95]

After the Second World War, Tetley assumed a new role. He joined the cast of *The Phil Harris-Alice Faye Show*, back when it was known as *The Fitch Bandwagon*. He took on the role of Julius Abbruzio, a mischievous and witty delivery boy for the local grocery store. During the early years of the show, the Julius character was a source of annoyance for star Phil Harris. It seemed that Abbruzio had developed a schoolboy crush on Alice and was always attempting to persuade Miss Faye to elope with him. When Phil and Alice's show switched sponsorship to Rexall, Julius transformed into "Leroy on steroids."[96] However, it was easy to tell them apart because Julius had a strong Bronx accent. He often played the devilish and spiteful nemesis to Harris and his guitar-playing friend Frankie Remley played by Elliot Lewis. Julius was always on the lookout for a way to ruin the duo's latest scheme. His romantic overtures to Mrs. Harris became a bit more blatant as well. But Phil, Frankie, and Julius were a comedic trio that delivered some of the finest moments in radio history. Tetley continued playing the role until the show signed off in 1954.[97]

---

[95] Shreve, Ivan G. "Happy Birthday, Walter Tetley!"
[96] Shreve, Ivan G. "Happy Birthday, Walter Tetley!"
[97] Shreve, Ivan G. "Happy Birthday, Walter Tetley!"

Throughout the postwar years, Walter found himself with a jam-packed schedule. He had a significant part in a syndicated transcription show called *The Anderson Family*, along with his network assignments.[98]

Back in the late 1920s, before the advent of tape recorders, digital delay, and computer playout options, the radio networks faced the challenge of ensuring that their programs aired at the correct time in every time zone.

Back in the early days, every program was performed live, often with multiple performances. One of the primary factors behind this decision was the desire of those on the West Coast to have the program begin three hours later than its original broadcast time to accommodate the time zone differences.

The costs can quickly add up when paying the talented individuals involved in the production, including the performers, announcers, musicians, and the dedicated team of professionals who provide support. The solution involved recording the program on acetate-based discs known as "electrical transcriptions" or ETs. That's why when you tune in to an old-time radio show, you might hear the announcer mention at the beginning of the program that the show has been "transcribed."[99]

Walter was eventually presented with a chance to host his very own network series titled *The Kid on The Corner*. The show would have showcased Tetley as a resourceful newsboy, sharing the spotlight with the seasoned announcer Harry Von Zell in a more serious role. In 1948, a

---
[98] McLeod, Elizabeth. "Eternal Youth: Walter Tetley, Radio's Essential Kid."
[99] Mishkind, Barry. "The Story behind: 'Transcribed.'" The Broadcasters Desktop Resource, 29 Feb. 2024.

recording of an audition was circulated, but sadly, it didn't catch the attention of any interested parties willing to sponsor it.[100]

At one point, Tetley experimented with voicing animated characters. In 1936, he provided his voice for *Felix the Cat* in a revival of the beloved 1920s character, but it failed to gain traction. In the 1940s, he frequently lent his voice to Andy Panda and a variety of other characters at the Walter Lantz studio.[101]

"Reddy Made Magic," a short film made by Lantz and Reddy Kilowatt creator Ashton B. Collins, Sr., was released in 1946. Tetley voiced Reddy Kilowatt, the spokesman for electricity generation, and performed the film's theme song. In 1959, he reprised his role in a remake called "The Mighty Atom," produced by John Sutherland.[102]

Walter's voice gained recognition among a new generation during the late 1950s and early 1960s. He was known as the voice behind Sherman, the nerdy, freckle-faced, bespectacled boy who served as the sidekick to the brilliant time-traveling dog, Mr. Peabody. In 1959, Sherman made his debut in the *Peabody's Improbable History* segments of Jay Ward's *Rocky and His Friends* (also known as *The Bullwinkle Show*).[103]

In the 1950s, Tetley worked for Capitol Records, where he used his voice to bring various characters to life on the label's spoken-word and comedy albums. One notable project he contributed to was *Stan Freberg Presents the United States of America Volume One: The Early Years* (1961). Harold Peary, his co-star on *The Great Gildersleeve* program, had

---

[100] McLeod, Elizabeth. "Eternal Youth: Walter Tetley, Radio's Essential Kid."
[101] McLeod, Elizabeth. "Eternal Youth: Walter Tetley, Radio's Essential Kid."
[102] "Walter Tetley." Wikipedia.
[103] "Walter Tetley." Wikipedia.

previously recorded three albums for Capitol in a style similar to Gildersleeve, where he narrated children's stories. [104]

Walter Tetley encountered numerous challenges during the late 1960s. Animation voice work was limited, and the call for fresh episodes was dwindling with each passing year due to the endless cycle of reruns. In addition, the radio industry was experiencing a decline and there were not many promising prospects in sight. Walter maintained a distance from his colleagues, finding it challenging to forge meaningful connections. Perhaps he took up motorcycling as a way to establish his independence and maturity, having spent so much of his professional life portraying child characters. In 1971, he was involved in a horrific accident that shattered his leg and required him to use a wheelchair for the rest of his life. Nevertheless, Walter persevered, lending his voice to commercials, television specials, and seizing every opportunity that came his way. In 1973, he was given a chance to once again step into the world of radio. Elliot Lewis contacted Tetley to discuss his participation in the upcoming *Hollywood Radio Theatre* series. It was to be Walter's last hoorah. In 1975, Walter Tetley passed away at the age of sixty due to complications from stomach cancer.[105]

---

[104] "Walter Tetley." Wikipedia.
[105] McLeod, Elizabeth. "Eternal Youth: Walter Tetley, Radio's Essential Kid."

xix. Lurene Tuttle, Dr. Christian publicity photo. Circa 1940. Public domain.

xx. Harold Peary, Walter Tetley and Lurene Tuttle publicity photo for The Great Gildersleeve. Public domain.

Lurene Tuttle

Marjorie Forrester (1941-1944)

Lurene Tuttle is well-known among radio enthusiasts for her memorable performances in two distinct roles. She portrayed the caring secretary Effie Perrine in *Sam Spade*, and she was the first actor to play Marjorie, the Great Gildersleeve's niece. However, Tuttle's impact went beyond the sum of her two well-known roles. She was a highly regarded personality in West Coast radio theater, having worked in the industry for many years. Furthermore, she played an important part in founding the first successful labor union in broadcasting.[106] She was also an avid Los Angeles Dodgers fan.

She was born in Indiana on August 29, 1907, into a family with a history in show business. Frank Tuttle, Lurene's grandfather, had a notable career as a drama instructor and opera house manager. Her father was a minstrel performer who had to find work selling railroad tickets after the popularity of the controversial, black-faced comedy shows declined in the 1890s. Lurene took to acting, following in the footsteps of her father and grandfather, and as a child she insisted on performing at every gathering whether or not anyone wanted to watch her.[107] When she was fifteen years old, she and her family moved to California, where she excelled in performing. She was involved in the school drama society and managed

---

[106] McLeod, Elizabeth. "Afra's First Lady: The Career of Lurene Tuttle." Radio Classics, 29 Aug. 2015.
[107] "Fifteen Cent-World Radio History." World Radio History, Jan. 1945.

to make a strong impression on the manager of the renowned Pasadena Playhouse, a highly regarded institution for semi-professional theater.[108]

Through her time as a stock actor in the Playhouse, she gained a profound grasp of the art of acting. Although she was only twenty years old, she had already amassed a wealth of experience in the world of acting. After a brief period in vaudeville, she decided to explore different opportunities in the early 1930s.[109]

At the time, radio's popularity was surging and the West Coast was becoming the hub of innovative and bold theatrical experimentation. Lindsay MacHarrie, a producer at Los Angeles station KHJ, carefully selected a talented group of actors who had demonstrated their skills in local theater productions and on the CBS network. After becoming a member of KHJ, Lurene quickly adapted to the atmosphere and demonstrated her impressive range as a performer by effortlessly taking on different roles. KHJ was well-known for its rigorous rehearsal schedules and its commitment to maintaining high performance standards for its actors. However, the artists were only paid for the live broadcasts and not for the extensive rehearsals.[110] Despite Lurene's dedicated efforts and considerable time commitment to her art, both she and her colleague Frank Nelson acknowledged the necessity to go beyond mere survival. Lurene and Frank believed they deserved a fair salary, respectable working conditions, and professional recognition.

They worked together on *Hollywood Hotel*, a highly acclaimed program on CBS. The sponsor, Campbell Soup, generously compensated the guest

---

[108] McLeod, Elizabeth. "Afra's First Lady: The Career of Lurene Tuttle."
[109] McLeod, Elizabeth. "Afra's First Lady: The Career of Lurene Tuttle."
[110] McLeod, Elizabeth. "Afra's First Lady: The Career of Lurene Tuttle."

stars and host Louella Parsons on a weekly basis. However, the actors who played supporting roles were paid very little.[111] Nelson and Tuttle both attempted to negotiate a $35 per performance increase. They were successful and the negotiations served as an incentive for them to establish a professional actors' union.[112]

Ultimately, more than one hundred radio actors in Los Angeles came together to establish the Radio Actors' Guild, which subsequently evolved into the first chapter of the American Federation of Radio Artists (AFRA). Lurene Tuttle was a founding member of that chapter and continued to be a committed union activist until her death.[113]

Over the next decade, Lurene Tuttle made a name for herself in the broadcasting industry, demonstrating her skills in various roles. She frequently appeared on the popular *Lux Radio Theatre*, often in minor roles, alongside numerous famous film actors. During her tenure on the show, she met Melville Ruick, the announcer for *Lux Radio Theatre*, who would eventually become her husband. By 1941, when she assumed the character of Marjorie Forrester on *The Great Gildersleeve*, she was in her late thirties, an experienced veteran actor portraying a teenage role.[114]

Lurene's straightforward portrayal of the character embodied a level of maturity that was unmatched by any of her successors in the role. She projected a firm authority as the lady of the house that prevented even her pompous uncle from overstepping his bounds. She brought a sense of dignity to the character of Marjorie, which was a refreshing departure

---

[111] McLeod, Elizabeth. "Afra's First Lady: The Career of Lurene Tuttle."
[112] Lurene Tuttle." Wikipedia.
[113] McLeod, Elizabeth. "Afra's First Lady: The Career of Lurene Tuttle."
[114] McLeod, Elizabeth. "Afra's First Lady: The Career of Lurene Tuttle."

from the typical portrayals of young women during that time.[115] The only source of worry for her devoted uncle was her remarkable talent for attracting countless boyfriends.

At the beginning of the series, Marjorie developed a romantic interest in Ted Wills, a charismatic and young attorney who served as a junior member of the law firm responsible for managing the Forrester estate. Another of her acquaintances was Oliver Honeywell, a hypochondriac. Oliver, known for his eccentricity and unpredictability, once requested permission to stay the night due to unexpected rain. He had forgotten his raincoat and wanted to avoid catching a chill on the streetcar. Oliver was not a serious contender in the romance department due to his numerous phobias and complexes, and the character was ultimately written off after only a few appearances.[116]

Oliver was replaced by Ben Waterford, whom everyone promptly christened "Bashful Ben." He was a talented mechanic and Gildersleeve frequently sought his assistance in performing necessary automotive repairs. When World War II broke out, Ben enlisted in the Navy, which temporarily halted their romance. Afterwards, he returned to Summerfield and managed a gas station, maintaining a close relationship with the family.[117]

Lurene Tuttle also ventured into the world of cinema and went on to establish a prolific career in television, portraying a variety of character roles for a span of thirty years. However, she was unable to establish the same level of versatility on television that she had in radio. A middle-

---
[115] McLeod, Elizabeth. "Afra's First Lady: The Career of Lurene Tuttle."
[116] Stumpf, Charles, and Ben Ohmart. "The Great Gildersleeve."
[117] Stumpf, Charles, and Ben Ohmart. "The Great Gildersleeve."

aged woman would never be able to give a nuanced portrayal of an eighteen-year-old girl in a visual medium. During her television career, she frequently took on roles of nurses, teachers, or mothers. Additionally, she portrayed gossipy small-town meddlers. She appeared in a variety of genres, including courtroom dramas, Westerns, and situation comedies. Her television career continued until the mid-1980s.[118]

Tuttle eventually married Melville Ruick. The pair had a daughter named Barbara (1932-1974), who later married film composer John Williams. Barbara pursued a career in the performing arts, following the path set by her mother, excelling in both acting and singing. Regrettably, her life was tragically cut short at the young age of forty-one due to a ruptured aneurysm.[119] Lurene and Mel divorced and on November 27, 1950, Lurene married Frederick W. Cole, an engineer. She filed for divorce from him on January 4, 1956.[120]

Throughout her acting career, she consistently demonstrated her passion for teaching and coaching. Even at the peak of her own success, she dedicated herself to helping others in the industry. An example of her commitment was when she provided guidance and training to radio actors who had taken a break from their craft to serve in World War II.[121]

Lurene had a passion for collecting a delightful assortment of canine figurines. The article "Toy Dogs, Not Real Ones, Are Actress' Hobby" was published in the *Oakland Tribune* on May 6, 1930. According to the

---

[118] McLeod, Elizabeth. "Afra's First Lady: The Career of Lurene Tuttle."
[119] "Barbara Ruick." Wikipedia, Wikimedia Foundation, 7 Apr. 2024.
[120] Lurene Tuttle." Wikipedia.
[121] Lurene Tuttle." Wikipedia.

article, Lurene had a collection of over two hundred miniature dog figurines displayed on her dressing room shelf."[122]

On May 28, 1986, Lurene Tuttle sadly lost her battle with cancer at a hospital in Encino, California. Howard Duff, who co-starred with her in *Sam Spade*, delivered a heartfelt eulogy in which he fondly remembered Lurene as follows:

"She could just take hold of a part and do something with it...I think she never met a part she didn't like. She just loved to work; she loved to act. She's a woman who was born to do what she was doing and loved every minute of it." [123]

---

[122] Lurene Tuttle." Wikipedia.
[123] Lurene Tuttle." Wikipedia.

xxi. Leroy, Gildersleeve, and Marjorie (Lurene Tuttle). Circa 1940s. Public domain.

xxii. Gildersleeve, Leroy, and Marjorie (Louise Erickson). Circa 1940s. Public domain.

Louise Erickson

Marjorie Forrester (1944-1948)

Louise Erickson, an American actress known for her work in radio and film, was born in Oakland, California on February 28, 1928. Her talent was in high demand during the 1940s, particularly for radio productions that required a teenage girl character. Louise was the star of *A Date with Judy*, a comedy radio series aimed at a teenage audience, from 1943 to 1950.[124] She took over the part of Marjorie Forrester from Lurene Tuttle, who played the character from 1941 to 1944. Louise greatly cherished her role on *The Great Gildersleeve*, although *A Date with Judy* catapulted her to radio stardom. She later reflected on her time on the series, stating, "Of all the programs I did on radio *The Great Gildersleeve* is the one that still stands up today; the writing was superb, and Hal Peary was a comedic genius."[125]

As the series progressed, with Louise taking on the role, Marjorie's character went through a remarkable change, becoming more like your average teenager. Despite her uncle's disapproval, she found herself completely fascinated by Marshall Bullard, the son of their wealthy and utterly insufferable neighbor Rumson Bullard, who moved into the neighborhood in 1945. Marshall's father also voiced his displeasure with the relationship, which finally led to the decision to enroll the young man in a prestigious East Coast preparatory school.[126]

---

[124] "A Date with Judy." Wikipedia, Wikimedia Foundation, 14 July 2024.
[125] Shreve, Ivan G. "Happy Birthday, Louise Erickson!" Radio Classics, 28 Feb. 2020.
[126] Stumpf, Charles, and Ben Ohmart. "The Great Gildersleeve."

Louise's father, Arthur Erickson, was a restauranteur who moved his family to Hollywood in 1935 when she was only seven years old. Louise's mother supported her daughter's ambition to pursue a career in show business, yet she was never the archetypal show business parent. Initially, she had hoped for Louise's brother to pursue a career in show business. He had played the violin, yet he never truly expressed a desire for a career on stage. Focusing her efforts on Louise's career instead, her mother penned letters to secure auditions for her and drove her to work until she was old enough to drive herself. Louise was fortunate enough to secure a highly sought-after part on a beloved local children's show known as *Uncle Whoa Bill*. Here, she skillfully portrayed a whimsical fairy princess, capturing the hearts of young viewers. When Louise was just thirteen years old, she captivated audiences with her incredible performance on network radio in the popular medical drama series *Dr. Christian*. Erickson also had the opportunity to showcase her talent on popular shows like *The Cavalcade of America* and *Mutual's Dramas of Youth*.[127]

She first appeared on the show *A Date with Judy* in the role of Mitzi, Judy Foster's confidante and partner in crime. Sponsored by Pepsodent and broadcast on NBC from June 24 to September 16, 1941, *A Date with Judy* began as a summer replacement for Bob Hope's program. Initially it featured fourteen-year-old Ann Gillis in the lead role and Mercedes McCambridge as Judy's girlfriend.[128] During the golden age of radio, many popular radio shows would go on a seasonal break. To keep the airwaves alive, networks would introduce summer replacement shows.

---

[127] Shreve, Ivan G. "Happy Birthday, Louise Erickson!"
[128] "A Date with Judy." Wikipedia.

This gave well-known radio personalities a chance to rest and provided aspiring stars with an opportunity to make their mark in the entertainment industry.

In the following summer season (June 23 - September 15, 1942), Dellie Ellis (later known as Joan Lorring) took on the role of Judy Foster, while Louise portrayed Mitzi. In the summer of 1943, Louise Erickson, who was only fifteen years old at the time, stepped into the spotlight. The series, now sponsored by Bristol Myers, became a summer replacement for *The Eddie Cantor Show*. Louise faithfully portrayed the character for an incredible seven-year period. She began her portrayal on NBC on January 18, 1944, and continued until January 4, 1949. Later, when the show moved to ABC, she carried on her role from October 13, 1949, to May 4, 1950.[129]

A Date with Judy opened the door to numerous opportunities in the radio industry. Prior to Janet Waldo assuming the role of the cheerful Emmy Lou on *The Adventures of Ozzie & Harriet*, Louise portrayed the character. Following the success of *A Date with Judy*, CBS decided to create their own teenage girl comedy called *Meet Corliss Archer*. Erickson had the opportunity to be on the show as Corliss' friend Mildred, with Corliss being portrayed by Janet Waldo. Janet subsequently depicted Leroy's music teacher and Gildy's romantic interest, Joanne Piper, in *The Great Gildersleeve* series. Louise later portrayed Babs, the eldest daughter of Chester A. Riley, a dim-witted blue-collar worker, on *The Life of Riley* throughout the show's duration. Erickson also made appearances on *The Adventures of the Saint*, *The Alan Young Show*, *Arch*

---

[129] "A Date with Judy." Wikipedia.

Oboler's Plays, *Cloak and Dagger*, *Granby's Green Acres*, *The Lady Esther Screen Guild Theatre*, *The Phil Harris-Alice Faye Show*, and *Repeat Performance*.[130]

After Lurene Tuttle departed from *The Great Gildersleeve* program in 1944, Louise auditioned for the character of Marjorie and was awarded the role. Similar to Hal and Lillian, she was also given the chance to sing on the show. Louise sang just one song, "It Might As Well Be Spring." After four short years, Hal dismissed Louise without providing an explanation. She thought that perhaps he objected to her having her own show, *A Date with Judy*. Despite her objections, Louise's mother was adamant that she write a letter to Hal, expressing her apologies. She made the effort, but it did not result in her getting her job back.

Louise's extensive experience in radio as Judy Foster would later allow her to transition to the film industry. Louise had a minor part in the 1944 musical comedy *Rosie the Riveter*, with Carl "Alfalfa" Switzer portraying her brother. In the film *Meet Miss Bobby Socks*, which was also released in the same year, she gained more attention for her portrayal of an infatuated teenager who develops strong feelings for a bandleader, played by Bob Crosby. In 1944, Louise made an appearance alongside Harold Peary in one of Paramount's "Unusual Occupations" short films. The segment provided a brief glimpse into the behind-the-scenes process of *The Great Gildersleeve* program. Louise was disappointed when MGM chose to adapt *A Date with Judy* into a film in 1948, with Jane Powell

---

[130] Shreve, Ivan G. "Happy Birthday, Louise Erickson!"

taking on the role of Judy. Her only other notable film is *Three Husbands* in 1950, in which she had a small yet memorable role.[131]

Following her stint in radio, Louise made the bold decision to move to New York and pursue her passion for theater. In 1957, she took to the stage for the first time, portraying the character Tina in the Broadway production of *A Hole in the Head*. Her acting career came to an end in 2009, when she shifted her focus to writing.[132] She pursued a multitude of writing assignments with PR firms putting together recipes and writing articles related to food.

Louise Erickson was married to the renowned actor Ben Gazzara. The couple met at the Dramatic Workshop located in Midtown Manhattan. Erickson introduced him to the Actors Studio, and in 1951, he successfully passed the audition. They got married in the same year but divorced in 1957.[133] While working at *Good Housekeeping*, Louise met art director Herb Leibowitz. They later married and had two sons.[134]

Louise Erickson passed away on March 18, 2019, at the age of ninety-one.[135]

---

[131] Shreve, Ivan G. "Happy Birthday, Louise Erickson!"
[132] Stumpf, Charles, and Ben Ohmart. "The Great Gildersleeve."
[133] Genzlinger, Neil. "Ben Gazzara, Risk-Taking Actor, Is Dead at 81." The New York Times, The New York Times, 3 Feb. 2012.
[134] Stumpf, Charles, and Ben Ohmart. "The Great Gildersleeve."
[135] "Louise Erickson (Actress)." Wikipedia, Wikimedia Foundation, 1 Mar. 2024.

xxiii. Mary Lee Robb, early 1940s. Public domain.

Mary Lee Robb
Marjorie Forrester (1948-1954)

When Louise Erickson was unable to attend the dress rehearsal of *The Great Gildersleeve*, Mary Lee Robb graciously stepped in as a substitute. Robb's exceptional talent secured her the coveted role of Marjorie for the highly anticipated autumn 1948 season.[136]

Robb had already established herself on radio when she landed the role of Marjorie. In 1947, she made her first appearance on the *Lum 'n' Abner* program, marking the beginning of her radio career.[137] She was selected to portray Pearl, the daughter of Abner Peabody. During a 1988 interview with author-historian Chuck Schaden on *Speaking of Radio*, Robb recalled her brief lines as Pearl: "I do," and "Don't cry, Papa." The episode featured Pearl's wedding. Mary Lee made $45 from reciting those two lines, but unfortunately, she had to pay a $75 fee to join the radio actors' union. Luckily, the actress would be able to participate in more radio projects in the years to come.[138]

Occasionally, she would mimic the sounds of the infant for little Robespierre, who was the younger brother of Snooks Higgins on Fanny Brice's *The Baby Snooks Show*. She had a recurring role on *Maxwell House Coffee Time* as Emily Vanderlipp, the teenage girl who lived next door to George Burns and Gracie Allen. Richard Crenna took on the role of Emily's boyfriend in George and Gracie's half-hour show, and later

---

[136] Shreve, Ivan G. "Happy Birthday, Louise Erickson!"
[137] Mary Lee Robb." Wikipedia, Wikimedia Foundation, 15 Aug. 2024.
[138] "Mary Lee Robb Cline, 80; Played Gildy's Niece on 'the Great Gildersleeve.'" Los Angeles Times, Los Angeles Times, 8 Sept. 2006.

became Marjorie's husband in *The Great Gildersleeve*. Robb had an impressive resume that highlighted her extensive experience in a wide range of productions, including *Family Theatre, Father Knows Best, Fibber McGee and Molly, The Railroad Hour, Red Ryder, This is Your FBI*,[139] and *The Penny Singleton Show*.[140]

Mary Lee Robb was born in Streator, Illinois, on February 15, 1926, to Alex S. Robb, an NBC executive, and his wife Madeleine Bourg Robb. In 1939, the family relocated to Los Angeles, where Mary Lee attended University High School. She decided to continue her education at UCLA after graduating, but in her sophomore year, she left to pursue a career in radio acting full-time. During her time studying drama at UCLA, Robb also gained valuable experience in radio performance at the Geller Radio Workshop, which was previously known as the Max Reinhardt Workshop. Louise Erickson was a fellow student at the Geller Workshop.[141]

Mary Lee was initially hired to participate in "off-mic babble" for the Gildersleeve program, where actors would gather around a microphone to create "crowd noises." Then came the fateful day when Erickson was running behind schedule and it appeared that she would miss the crucial dress rehearsal. Robb volunteered to take on the responsibility of reading the Marjorie part to ensure precise timing of the broadcast. For a brief moment, it appeared that Mary Lee might need to step in on the air due to Louise's tardiness. Fortunately, Louise made it to the show just in time, five minutes before it started. However, Mary Lee's portrayal as a

---

[139] Shreve, Ivan G. "Happy Birthday, Mary Lee Robb!" Radio Spirits, 15 Feb. 2020.
[140] "Mary Lee Robb." Wikipedia.
[141] "Mary Lee Robb Cline, 80; Played Gildy's Niece on 'the Great Gildersleeve.'" Los Angeles Times.

"temporary Marjorie" left such a positive impact that when Louise departed from *The Great Gildersleeve* at the end of the 1947-48 season, the show's creators chose Robb as her successor.[142]

Mary Lee Robb was particularly fond of the episode in which Marjorie became Mrs. Bronco Thompson. The cast went all out for the May 10, 1950 event, dressing up in full wedding regalia for the studio audience. In an article titled "Gildersleeve Gives the Bride Away" published on May 23, *Look* magazine showcased the Gildersleeve cast as they prepared for the nuptials.[143]

Mary Lee continued to participate in the Gildersleeve program until 1954, when she retired from the entertainment industry following the birth of her daughter, Alexandra.[144]

Robb and Charles Vance Smith were married in 1952. The couple had two children, a daughter and a son, but unfortunately, their marriage ended in divorce. In 1983, she married William H. Cline. Cline passed away in October 2005, ending their twenty-two-year marriage.[145]

Mary Lee Robb passed away on August 28, 2006, from heart failure at Desert Regional Medical Center in Palm Springs. She had been a member of The Pacific Pioneer Broadcasters for an extended period of time and had participated in numerous panels and recreations, such as the Radio Hall of Fame and SPERDVAC. Mary Lee was both pleased and astonished by the resurgence of interest in old-time radio programs.[146]

---

[142] Shreve, Ivan G. "Happy Birthday, Mary Lee Robb!"
[143] Shreve, Ivan G. "Happy Birthday, Mary Lee Robb!"
[144] Shreve, Ivan G. "Happy Birthday, Mary Lee Robb!"
[145] "Mary Lee Robb Cline, 80; Played Gildy's Niece on 'the Great Gildersleeve.'"
[146] Mary Cline Obituary (2006) - Palm Springs, CA - The Desert Sun." Legacy.Com, Legacy, 12 Sept. 2006.

xxiv. Walter Tetley, Harold Peary, Mary Lee Robb, and Jeanette Nolan. Public domain.

xxv. Gildersleeve gives away the bride from LOOK Magazine May 23, 1950 pictorial feature. Public domain.

xxvi. Lillian Randolph on The Beulah Show. Cicra 1952. Public domain.

Lillian Randolph

Allegedly, upon hearing about the auditions for the Gildersleeve program, Lillian quickly made her way to NBC. She dashed through the winding corridors, heart pounding with anticipation. Finally reaching the entrance to the studio, she stumbled and crashed to the ground, her face meeting the cold, unforgiving floor. Luckily, she came out of it without any harm, and her contagious laughter ultimately landed her the part of Birdie. [147]

Lillian Randolph had a remarkable career as an actress, captivating audiences on the airwaves, silver screen, and television with her immense talent. Throughout her career, she consistently and confidently brought to life the character of the Black domestic in film and radio. She passionately defended her choice to portray such characters, resolute in her convictions. [148]

Her birth name was Castello Randolph and she was born in Knoxville, Tennessee on December 14, 1898. She and her sister Amanda Randolph, who also gained recognition as an actress, were born to a Methodist minister and a teacher. Lillian started her professional career on the radio circuits in Cleveland and Detroit. [149] While working at WXYZ in Detroit, she caught the attention of George W. Trendle, the manager of the station and the creator of *The Lone Ranger*. He enrolled her for radio training courses, which enabled her to secure roles on various local radio programs. Interestingly, Randolph underwent three months of training

---

[147] "Lillian Randolph." Wikipedia.
[148] Wartts, Adrienne. "Lillian Randolph (1915-1980)." Black Past, 10 Dec. 2020.
[149] Williams, Rachelle. "Lillian Randolph: A Prolific Black Actress of the Classic Film and TV Era." Reel Rundown, 15 Mar. 2023.

with a Caucasian actor, where the focus was on racial dialect, before she was able to find any work on radio.[150]

In 1936, Randolph relocated to Los Angeles and made her first appearance as a singer at the Club Alabam. She also worked in radio on Al Jolson's *The Lifebuoy Show*, *Big Town*, and the *Al Pearce Show*.[151] Five years later, she successfully secured the role of Birdie, the maid, in the radio and TV series *The Great Gildersleeve*, which propelled her to become one of the most sought-after Black actresses of that era. Randolph depicted the character of Birdie until 1957.[152]

Birdie was never hesitant to express her thoughts, yet she consistently did so in a considerate manner. Wherever she happened to be in the house, she would always eagerly respond with, "I'll get it!" whenever the phone rang or someone appeared at the door. Unfortunately, it was often the case that someone else managed to get it before she had the chance.

Since the day Marjorie and Leroy entered this world, Birdie had been their devoted caretaker, attending to their every need with affection. The Forrester children were born into a life of privilege, thanks to their father, Charles, who successfully ran a car dealership and a real estate agency. The kind-hearted housekeeper provided invaluable assistance to Marjorie, guiding her through the ups and downs of her teenage love life. She also had a remarkable ability to instill discipline in Leroy whenever he misbehaved, all while remaining calm and composed.[153]

Lillian concurrently portrayed the character of Daisy, the housekeeper on *The Billie Burke Show* from 1943 to 1946. In the early 1950s she was

---

[150] "Lillian Randolph." Wikipedia.
[151] "Lillian Randolph." Wikipedia.
[152] Wartts, Adrienne. "Lillian Randolph (1915-1980)."
[153] Stumpf, Charles, and Ben Ohmart. "The Great Gildersleeve."

given the lead role in the radio program *Beulah,* replacing actress Hattie McDaniel. Lillian portrayed Beulah for a year before passing the role on to her sister, Amanda. She also appeared on the *Amos 'n' Andy* television program, where she reprised her role as Madame Queen, a character she originally portrayed on the radio version of the series.[154]

The Randolph sisters never stopped looking for ways to make ends meet. However, in 1938, Lillian kindly welcomed Lena Horne into her home while the latter was in California for her debut film, *The Duke Is Tops* (1938). Because of the film's tight budget, Horne couldn't afford to stay at a hotel. Lillian Randolph was also known for her generous spirit during World War II, as she hosted weekly dinners and organized entertainment for service people in the Los Angeles area. She worked closely with the American Women's Voluntary Services to make these events possible.[155]

Despite her friendly nature, Lillian faced criticism for her voice-over roles as a maid in several Hanna-Barbera cartoon shorts. The NAACP expressed their discontent with her and Hanna-Barbera due to the prominent portrayal of offensive racial stereotypes in the cartoons. Consequently, the studio made the choice to remove the character from the films.[156] Lillian received similar criticism in 1946 from *Ebony* magazine for her portrayal of Birdie on *The Great Gildersleeve* radio program. She offered the critics an alternative perspective, as did the show's writer Sam Moore. The reputation and prospects for African

---

[154] Wartts, Adrienne. "Lillian Randolph (1915-1980)."
[155] "Lillian Randolph." Wikipedia.
[156] Williams, Rachelle. "Lillian Randolph: A Prolific Black Actress of the Classic Film and TV Era."

Americans in the future, in Randolph's opinion, were unaffected by these roles.[157]

Two of Randolph's most well-known movie roles were Annie in *It's a Wonderful Life* (1946) and Bessie in *The Bachelor and the Bobby-Soxer* (1947). In 1969, she went on to play Bill Cosby's mother in the renowned television series *The Bill Cosby Show*. Lillian was the first African American to serve on the Board of Directors for the Hollywood chapter of the American Federation of Television and Radio Artists (AFTRA).[158]

The actress had four marriages throughout her lifetime. She adopted a daughter named Barbara during her third marriage to Edward Sanders. For a short while, Barbara Randolph—better known as Barbara Ann Sanders—followed in her mother's footsteps as an actress. She starred alongside Harry Belafonte and Dorothy Dandridge in *Bright Road* (1953) and with Sidney Poitier, Spencer Tracy, Katherine Hepburn, and then-rising black actress Isabel Sanford of *The Jeffersons* in "Guess Who's Coming to Dinner" (1967). Barbara Ann gave up acting to pursue her passion of singing, and through her records for Motown and RCA, she became a well-known name in the music business.[159]

In her later years, Lillian went back to singing the blues. In addition, she scored a part in the television miniseries *Roots* (1977) and had notable appearances on classic TV shows like *Sanford and Son* and *The Jeffersons*. She also instructed aspiring young actors in the art of acting,

---

[157] Wartts, Adrienne. "Lillian Randolph (1915-1980)."
[158] Williams, Rachelle. "Lillian Randolph: A Prolific Black Actress of the Classic Film and TV Era."
[159] Williams, Rachelle. "Lillian Randolph: A Prolific Black Actress of the Classic Film and TV Era."

guiding them towards their dreams of fame in Hollywood. The Black Filmmakers Hall of Fame inducted Randolph in March 1980.[160]

The entertainment world said good-bye to Lillian on September 12, 1980. She was eighty-one. Lillian and her sister Amanda are buried next to each other at the Forest Lawn Memorial Park in the Hollywood Hills.[161]

---

[160] Williams, Rachelle. "Lillian Randolph: A Prolific Black Actress of the Classic Film and TV Era."
[161] Williams, Rachelle. "Lillian Randolph: A Prolific Black Actress of the Classic Film and TV Era."

xxvii. Richard Crenna. A Date with Judy. Public domain.

Richard Crenna

Richard Crenna enjoyed an exceptionally long and successful career spanning over sixty-five years, during which he portrayed unforgettable characters across various mediums such as radio, television, and film. Having started his radio career at the tender age of eleven, he continued to act on television until his passing.[162]

Richard Donald Crenna was born to Edith and Domenick Crenna in Los Angeles on November 30, 1926. He developed a passion for radio acting during his time at Belmont Senior High School, which ultimately resulted in him securing a role on the *Boy Scout Jamboree* program. After completing his education, Crenna joined the United States Army and served as a radioman during World War II. He played a prominent role in military operations, including major battles like The Battle of the Bulge and engagements in the Pacific Theater. Following the war, he decided to pursue a degree in English at the University of Southern California. In addition, he remained involved in radio and gained recognition for his performance as Oogie Pringle, the quirky boyfriend of the main character on the critically acclaimed show *A Date with Judy*.[163] Crenna's other early acting experiences included portraying the awkward high-school character Walter Denton on *Our Miss Brooks*, appearing on both radio and television.[164] Richard later secured a recurring role on *The Great Gildersleeve* as Walter "Bronco" Thompson, Marjorie's boyfriend.

---

[162] "Irreplaceable Richard Crenna." Legacy.Com, 17 Jan. 2013.
[163] Shreve, Ivan G. "Happy Birthday, Richard Crenna!" Radio Spirits RSS, 30 Nov. 2014.
[164] "Irreplaceable Richard Crenna." Legacy.Com.

Bronco was friendly and easygoing, but a bit bashful. It took some time for him to muster enough courage to ask Marjorie out. Gildersleeve took an instant liking to him, and Bronco began spending a lot of time at their home. Birdie enjoyed cooking meals to accommodate his healthy appetite.[165]

After a long on-and-off courtship, Marjorie finally agreed to marry Bronco. With a date in mind, the journey ahead was not without its share of challenges. The bride's headstrong uncle and the groom's highly opinionated mother clashed with each other. Mrs. Thompson insisted on hosting the ceremony in her elegant residence in Broadmoor, disregarding Gildersleeve's proposal to have the couple wed in the comfort of their own home in Summerfield. Bronco's father made the choice to stay out of the argument.[166]

The in-laws' divergent viewpoints led to arguments about a number of wedding-related issues, such as the choice of flowers, the reception location, and the bride's dress design. Marjorie finally intervened and made it clear that she wanted wear her mother's wedding gown. It was one of the rare occasions on which the parents were mentioned.[167]

During the memorable May 10, 1950 broadcast, the couple exchanged their vows and became husband and wife.[168]

In addition to his role on *The Great Gildersleeve,* Richard made sporadic appearances on George Burns and Gracie Allen's show as a lovestruck teenager named Waldo. He also portrayed various characters on comedy

---

[165] Stumpf, Charles, and Ben Ohmart. "The Great Gildersleeve."
[166] Stumpf, Charles, and Ben Ohmart. "The Great Gildersleeve."
[167] Stumpf, Charles, and Ben Ohmart. "The Great Gildersleeve."
[168] Shreve, Ivan G. "Happy Birthday, Richard Crenna!"

programs such as *The Fabulous Dr. Tweedy*, *A Day in the Life of Dennis Day*, *My Favorite Husband*, and *The Hardy Family*. However, it was his portrayal of Walter Denton, Connie Brooks' student confidant on *Our Miss Brooks*, that catapulted Richard Crenna to radio immortality. [169]

Crenna's performance showcased his remarkable sense of comedic timing as he brought to life the well-meaning but socially awkward character. Walter's undying devotion to his beloved English teacher often caused him to clash with the strict school principal Conklin, portrayed by Gale Gordon. It is worth noting that Walter had a personal stake in these situations, as he was romantically involved with Conklin's daughter Harriet. [170] Crenna, along with the majority of the cast, made the transition when *Our Miss Brooks* became a smash on television. He also appeared in the 1956 film adaption of the series. [171]

Richard found himself in a bit of a dilemma when he auditioned for the sitcom that would later become his second successful television project, *The Real McCoys*. He had become so closely associated with the Walter Denton character that it posed a challenge for him. The producers of that famous series were in search of an actor with a more "masculine" image to play the role of Luke McCoy, instead of the geeky character Crenna popularized in *Our Miss Brooks*. Richard's image underwent a remarkable transformation, leading to his success on the program for a remarkable six seasons. [172]

---

[169] Shreve, Ivan G. "Happy Birthday, Richard Crenna!"
[170] Shreve, Ivan G. "Happy Birthday, Richard Crenna!"
[171] Shreve, Ivan G. "Happy Birthday, Richard Crenna!"
[172] Shreve, Ivan G. "Happy Birthday, Richard Crenna!"

After his time on *The Real McCoys*, he took on a fresh challenge: starring in a one-hour drama series as James Slattery, a state legislator, in *Slattery's People*. In spite of its critical acclaim during the 1964-65 season, the program failed to ignite much enthusiasm among the audience. The show was given a second season by CBS, only to be later canceled. However, Crenna's performance earned *Slattery's People* two Emmy Award nominations. Surprisingly, it wasn't until 1985 that the actor finally received an Emmy. This prestigious award was given to him in recognition of his outstanding performance in the TV-movie *The Rape of Richard Beck*.[173]

In the film, Crenna took on the role of veteran police detective Richard Beck, which was quite different from the characters he had previously portrayed. Beck often lacks empathy for victims of sex crimes, suggesting that they somehow brought it upon themselves. Nevertheless, following a traumatic incident involving two male suspects, Beck finds himself grappling with his own perspective as he delves into the investigation of his own rape case. Not only did Crenna take home the prestigious Emmy for Outstanding Lead Actor in a Limited Series or a Special, but he also received a well-deserved nomination for a Golden Globe Award for Best Performance by an Actor in a Mini-Series or Motion Picture Made for TV.[174]

Richard's extensive and varied film career was made possible by his work in radio and television. His filmography was filled with an eclectic mix of movies, from *The Sand Pebbles* and *The Flamingo Kid* to *Marooned, Body Heat*, and the timeless Audrey Hepburn classic *Wait Until Dark*.

---

[173] Shreve, Ivan G. "Happy Birthday, Richard Crenna!"
[174] "The Rape of Richard Beck." Wikipedia, Wikimedia Foundation, 1 Aug. 2024.

However, Crenna's most iconic role on the silver screen is Colonel Sam Troutman, the commanding officer of John Rambo in the first three Rambo movies. In a clever twist, he hilariously spoofed this character as Colonel Denton Walters, drawing inspiration for the name from the role he played on the radio, in the movie *Hot Shots! Part Deux*. Crenna rounded out his career with a recurring role on the television program *Judging Amy*, which marked his last performance. His character, Jared Duff, was written out when Crenna passed away at the age of seventy-six. [175] Richard Crenna, who was diagnosed with pancreatic cancer, passed away from heart failure at six p.m. on Friday, January 17, 2003, in the intensive care unit of Cedars-Sinai Medical Center.[176]

---

[175] "Irreplaceable Richard Crenna." Legacy.Com.
[176] "Actor Richard Crenna Dead at 76." CNN, Cable News Network, 22 Jan. 2003.

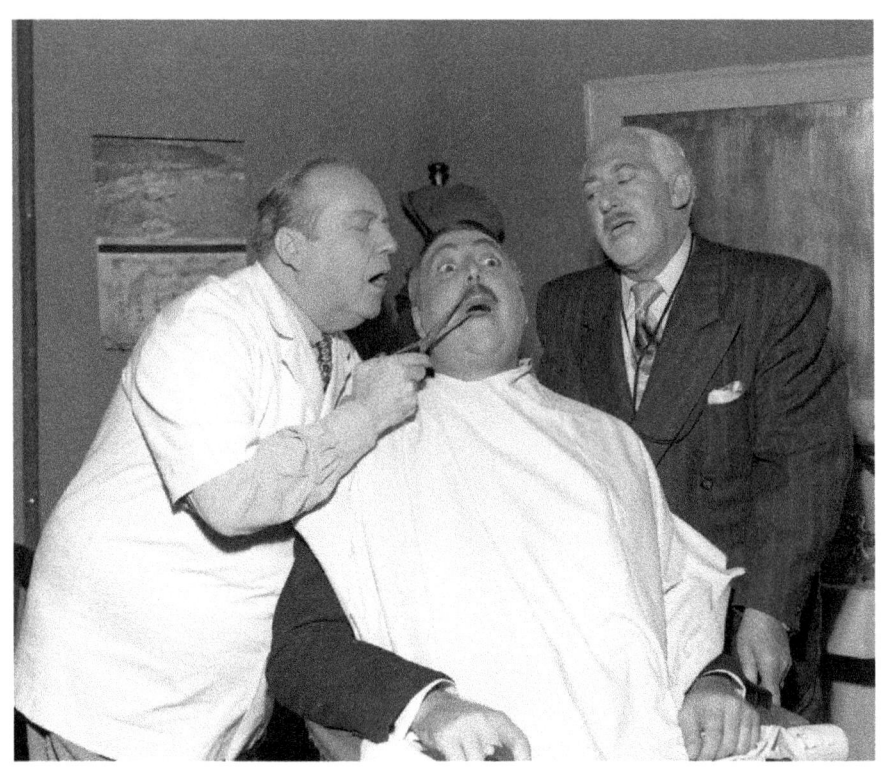

xxviii. Arthur Q. Bryan as Floyd Munson the barber, Willard Waterman as Throckmorton P. Gildersleeve and Earle Ross as Judge Hooker on The Great Gildersleeve. Public domain.

Earle Ross

Actor Earle Ross had a wonderful soprano voice when he was younger, and he made good use of it by singing in his local church's boys' choir. His parents had hoped that he would pursue a career in the ministry someday, but his life ended up taking a completely different direction. One day, in the midst of a performance, Earle's voice unexpectedly faltered when he reached for a high note. For several days, he found himself unable to utter a single word. After recovering his ability to speak, his voice had taken on a noticeably deeper tone. "The more I talked," Ross reminisced in later years, "the lower my voice seemed to get. I didn't sound like a boy anymore. I sounded like an old man."[177]

Ross was born in Chicago on March 29, 1888. He used his talent to build a successful career in show business, specializing in playing older characters. His performances as traditional authority figures were truly remarkable, but it is his unforgettable portrayal of Judge Hooker on the beloved radio sitcom *The Great Gildersleeve* that will forever resonate with radio enthusiasts.[178]

During Gildersleeve's train journey from Wistful Vista to Summerfield, he had his first encounter with the cantankerous old Judge Hooker. As luck would have it, the judge would oversee the responsibilities Gildersleeve was about to carry out for the estate. The unlikely pair had an instant dislike for each other. During the overnight train ride, Gildersleeve found himself seated across from the judge in the busy

---
[177] Shreve, Ivan G. "Happy Birthday, Earle Ross!" Radio Spirits, 29 Mar. 2019.
[178] Shreve, Ivan G. "Happy Birthday, Earle Ross!"

dining car. Insults were hurled back and forth, with numerous remarks targeting Gildersleeve's weight. Naturally, the last available spot in the sleeping car happened to be the one situated above the dreaded judge.[179]

The initial conflict between Gildersleeve and Judge Hooker in the early episodes, may have been seen as unsuitable for a comedy series. As a result, the writers and actors made efforts to soften the characters. There were still some lingering conflicts in the scripts, but future shows took on a more tranquil and relaxed tone.[180]

The judge began affectionately referring to his adversary as "Gildy." But, whenever Throckmorton encountered an intriguing woman, which seemed to happen quite frequently, Hooker would also become quite fixated on her.[181] After he had gotten a taste of Birdie's cooking, the judge frequently fenagled an invitation to dinner. Time and time again, he tried to persuade her to work for him, offering a lighter workload and better pay. Upon making this discovery, Gildersleeve couldn't help but exclaim, "That crook of a Hooker tried to hook our cook again!"[182]

Earle Ross' love for acting developed after his voice changed. He chose to depict older characters, often senior men or villains, rather than accepting the usual younger roles.[183] Ross started his career on the East Coast in 1912, appearing in both Broadway and off-Broadway productions like *Cost of Living* and *Where the Trail Divides*. Afterwards, Earle put his experience in stage management to good use and created a prosperous chain of theaters. Unfortunately, the business venture was

---

[179] Stumpf, Charles, and Ben Ohmart. The Great Gildersleeve.
[180] Stumpf, Charles, and Ben Ohmart. The Great Gildersleeve.
[181] Stumpf, Charles, and Ben Ohmart. The Great Gildersleeve.
[182] Stumpf, Charles, and Ben Ohmart. The Great Gildersleeve.
[183] Shreve, Ivan G. "Happy Birthday, Earle Ross!"

abruptly halted by the devastating stock market crash in 1929.[184] Undeterred, Ross quickly found acting opportunities for himself in the rapidly growing field of radio. In the late 1920s, he hosted his own program called *The Earle Ross Theatre of the Air*. He also appeared in an early radio series written by Carlton E. Morse, the creator of *One Man's Family*. In this series, Ross portrayed the character of Inspector Post. Earle, who was one of the pioneering members in Actors' Equity, was also featured in *The Ramblings of Jonathan Quid*, another early radio offering. Ross ultimately made his way onto network shows such as *The Lux Radio Theatre*, where he became a member of the program's unofficial stock company. Additionally, he worked on *The Columbia Workshop* and *Dr. Christian*. During this period, Earle began making regular appearances on the quirky comedy-drama *Point Sublime*, an enticing series that revolves around the love story of two of its residents: storekeeper/mayor Ben Willet (played by Cliff Arquette) and Evelyn "Evy" Hanover (played by Jane Morgan). Ross portrayed retired Texas industrialist Howie McBrayer, who served as Ben's adversary in the series.[185]

Earle Ross solidified his radio legacy by portraying Judge Horace Hooker on *The Great Gildersleeve*, where he faced off against another rival. Hooker was a cantankerous old codger whose arguments with Gildersleeve brought plenty of laughter to the listeners of the show. He earned the nickname "the old goat" from the water commissioner because of his distinctive Billy goat laugh. Judge Hooker and Gildersleeve often found themselves locked in witty banter, yet their friendship remained resilient. They eventually

---

[184] "Earle Ross." Wikipedia, Wikimedia Foundation, 1 Jan. 2024.
[185] Shreve, Ivan G. "Happy Birthday, Earle Ross!"

joined other Summerfield friends in the fraternal organization known as "The Jolly Boys."[186]

During the broadcast of *The Lady Esther Screen Guild Theatre* on August 13, 1945, Earle played the role of Judge Hooker in the program's adaptation of the 1943 film *Gildersleeve's Bad Day*. Nevertheless, Ross appeared in only one of the RKO films that were inspired by the Gildersleeve program, specifically the 1944 movie titled *Gildersleeve's Ghost*. In the other films, such as *Gildersleeve's Bad Day*, the character of Hooker was portrayed by Charles Arnt.[187]

Ross had recurring roles on several television shows, including Billie Burke's sitcom where he played the disapproving brother Julius, *The Mel Blanc Show* where he portrayed Uncle Rupert, and *Meet Millie* where he acted alongside Audrey Totter and Bea Benaderet as Millie's demanding boss, J.R. Boone Sr. Earle also showcased his comedic talent on various radio programs including *The Adventures of Maisie*, *Beulah*, *Father Knows Best*, *Fibber McGee and Molly*, *The Halls of Ivy*, *The Jack Benny Program*, *Life with Luigi*, *Maxwell House Coffee Time*, *Meet Corliss Archer*, *The Merry Life of Mary Christmas*, *Mr. and Mrs. Blandings*, *Our Miss Brooks*, *The Phil Harris-Alice Faye Show*, and *Shorty Bell*.[188]

Earle Ross has appeared in several films, including *The Courageous Dr. Christian* (1940) and *A Date with the Falcon* (1941). He is known to Western film enthusiasts as Professor Cleary in *Riders of the Whistling Skull* (1937).

---

[186] Shreve, Ivan G. "Happy Birthday, Earle Ross!"
[187] Shreve, Ivan G. "Happy Birthday, Earle Ross!"
[188] Shreve, Ivan G. "Happy Birthday, Earle Ross!"

Regrettably, Earle Ross' long career in entertainment came to an end on May 21, 1961, when he lost his battle with cancer. He was seventy-three.[189]

---

[189] Shreve, Ivan G. "Happy Birthday, Earle Ross!"

xxix. Richard LeGrand as Mr. Peavey. Public domain.

Richard LeGrand

When it comes to memorable characters on *The Great Gildersleeve*, one name that always comes up is "Mr. Peavey." Portrayed by character actor Richard LeGrand for most of the run, this character was consistently the subject of discussion. Mr. Peavey was the proud proprietor of Peavey's Drug Store in Summerfield. He was a man with a reserved demeanor and a dry, witty sense of humor. His vacillating response, "Well now, I wouldn't say that," was a catch-phrase used for many years.[190]

Despite Gildersleeve's larger-than-life persona, the spotlight never dimmed on the gifted ensemble of supporting characters, each bringing their own unique charm to the story. Among them, Mr. Peavey shone brightly, leaving a lasting impression on the audience. It seemed that Gildersleeve or his family would frequent the drug store situated on the corner of State Street and Parkside Avenue, often striking up conversations with the calm and knowledgeable pharmacist.[191]

But Peavey's role as Gildersleeve's pharmacist didn't come about right away. In the early stages of the series, when Gildersleeve suffered from an intractable case of hiccups, Marjorie suggested, "I'll bet Mr. Fowler at the drug store has something to help you."[192]

In August 1942, Mr. Peavey was introduced as a one-time character; however, his popularity was such that he was shortly added to the regular

---

[190] "Mr. Peavey." Media Heritage - Preserving Radio and Television History, 12 Mar. 2013.
[191] Lynch, Jacqueline T. "Richard LaGrand - Mr. Peavey and a Film Debut." Richard LaGrand - Mr. Peavey and a Film Debut, 23 May 2024.
[192] Smith, Mickey C. "Images of Pharmacy and Pharmacists in Old-Time Radio: A Profile of Richard Q. Peavey."

cast. Peavey was depicted as the hen-pecked husband of Mrs. Peavey.[193] He established his shop in 1921 and whenever a customer inquired about one of his products, his response was always the same, "Any particular kind you had in mind?"[194] Many times his clients merely stopped by to seek his philosophical advice. The drug store's popular soda fountain contributed significantly to its modest earnings.[195]

Mr. Peavey loved rhubarb and had a Studebaker that he kept on blocks. He frequented the movies several times during the year and enjoyed Parcheesi. He was an arts enthusiast who sang with the Jolly Boys and played the piccolo and violin.[196] Despite his persistent attempts, he frequently failed to persuade the group to participate in singing the 1883 folk song "There Is a Tavern in the Town."[197] The song served as the official anthem of Trinity University College. It was also performed by Rudy Vallée under the title "The Drunkard Song," with a slight alteration to the chorus.

There is a tavern in the town, in the town
And there my true love sits him down, sits him down,
And drinks his wine as merry as can be,
And never, never thinks of me.

Chorus: Fare thee well, for I must leave thee,
Do not let this parting grieve thee,

---

[193] "Mr. Peavey." Media Heritage - Preserving Radio and Television History.
[194] Stumpf, Charles, and Ben Ohmart. The Great Gildersleeve.
[195] Stumpf, Charles, and Ben Ohmart. The Great Gildersleeve.
[196] Smith, Mickey C. "Images of Pharmacy and Pharmacists in Old-Time Radio: A Profile of Richard Q. Peavey."
[197] "Richard Legrand." Wikipedia, Wikimedia Foundation, 3 June 2024.

And remember that the best of friends
Must part, must part.[198]

Mr. Peavey's wife had a rather imposing maiden name: Horsefall. They met at a community picnic while he was working as a salesman for a wholesale drug firm. After a while, when he proposed to her, she readily accepted. However, she quickly added that she would only agree to it once he had his own drugstore.

She called him daily at the pharmacy. He would politely answer the phone, "Hello, Mrs. Peavey. This is Mr. Peavey."[199] Every Easter, he would present her with a potted begonia, and without fail, she would scold him, reminding him of the impropriety of such extravagance.[200] Mrs. Peavey kept a parrot who only spoke French. Mr. Peavey ran away from home during the spring of 1947 because Mrs. Peavey kept the talkative bird in the bedroom at night, which prevented him from getting any sleep.[201]

Nevertheless, the actor who portrayed Mr. Richard Quincy Peavey was anything but a hen-pecked homebody. Clifford Richard Le Grand, born in Portland, Oregon on August 29, 1882, was characterized as a daring individual who, during his teenage years, embarked on a maritime journey as a deck-hand on a cargo vessel. LeGrand traveled extensively to several countries, but eventually established himself in the United States as a stagehand in a theater. In 1901, when an actor failed to show up for a role, LeGrand graciously stepped in to save the day. He reveled

---

[198] "There Is a Tavern in the Town." Wikipedia, Wikimedia Foundation, 4 July 2024.
[199] Stumpf, Charles, and Ben Ohmart. The Great Gildersleeve.
[200] Smith, Mickey C. "Images of Pharmacy and Pharmacists in Old-Time Radio: A Profile of Richard Q. Peavey."
[201] Stumpf, Charles, and Ben Ohmart. The Great Gildersleeve.

in the experience, which inspired him to embark on a career in acting during the early days of the traveling shows.²⁰²

In 1928, LeGrand began his radio career at the age of forty-six. He took on the role of Professor Knicklebine in a production titled *School Days* and lent his voice as an announcer for the *Pacific Vagabonds* program. The directors were amazed by his remarkable talent for dialects, which eventually landed him the role of Ole Swenson, the janitor at the Elks Club, on *Fibber McGee and Molly* as the show was beginning to wind down. There is a possibility this character was inspired by LeGrand's earlier radio show, *Ole and the Girls*. He remained committed to *Fibber McGee and Molly* throughout its fifteen-minute days.²⁰³ However, Mr. Peavey was undeniably LeGrand's most renowned role. Not only did he excel on radio, but he was also chosen to portray the character in three of the Great Gildersleeve films.²⁰⁴

In February 1951, Peavey was honored by the National Association of Retail Druggists as "America's Favorite Neighborhood Druggist," coinciding with his fiftieth anniversary in show business.²⁰⁵

---

²⁰² "Mr. Peavey." Media Heritage - Preserving Radio and Television History.
²⁰³ "Richard Legrand." Wistful Vista, sites.google.com/site/wistfulvistasite/wistful-vista/fibber-mcgee-and-molly/cast-and-crew/richard-legrand..
²⁰⁴ "Mr. Peavey." Media Heritage - Preserving Radio and Television History.
²⁰⁵ "Richard Legrand." Wikipedia.

xxx. Richard LeGrand and Harold Peary in Gildersleeve's Ghost (1944). Public domain.

xxxi. Forrest Lewis. Circa 1940. Public domain.

Forrest Lewis

During the last two years of the radio program, Forrest Lewis, a versatile actor renowned for his wide range of voices, portrayed Mr. Peavey the druggist. Lewis transitioned the role to television when *The Great Gildersleeve* was syndicated in 1954-1955. In addition, he played the uncredited role of druggist Carson in the film *Gildersleeve on Broadway* (1943).

Raymond Forrest Lewis was born on November 5, 1899, in Knightstown, Indiana. Through sheer necessity, he developed his vocal abilities when he became a part of a repertoire company that visited his hometown when he was just seventeen. Throughout his time with this company, he took on a multitude of roles that truly highlighted his adaptability.[206] Later, he ventured to Broadway, experiencing both triumphs and setbacks. One season, he found himself working alongside the incredibly talented Lenore Ulric, a renowned star of both Broadway and Hollywood during the silent-film and early sound era. Their collaboration in the mesmerizing production of *Lulu Belle* was highly successful. He participated in countless road shows of Broadway productions, leading up in his last performance in 1930 in *Broken Dishes*.[207]

After his time on Broadway, Lewis moved to Chicago and secured his first radio role. It was that of an old man. On September 1, 1948, Lewis stated in an interview with the *St. Louis Post-Dispatch*, "I played old men when I was young, and when I got older, they had me playing boys. That's

---

[206] Dickson, Terry. "Forrest Lewis." Newspapers.Com, St. Louis Post-Dispatch, 1 Sept. 1948.
[207] Dickson, Terry. "Forrest Lewis."

show business."[208] Lewis' radio credits include *Grand Hotel, First Nighter, Cavalcade of America, Story of Mary Marlin, One Man's Family, I Love a Mystery*, and *Tom Mix Ralston Straight Shooters*.[209]

On Tom Mix, he played a total of eighty-seven distinct characters and had nine recurring roles. Wash, a Black character; Doc Green, the village doctor; Angus McPhee, the bookstore proprietor; Patchwood, the hotel man; and several regulars, such as Colorado Money and assorted villains, were all portrayed by Lewis.[210]

Nevertheless, there were drawbacks to assuming the roles of multiple characters. Lewis was simultaneously portraying the characters of Wash, a Nazi, and an English inspector of police in a single episode of the program. He flipped the page over and discovered that the subsequent sequence of lines was not accompanied by any indication of the character who was speaking. He made an incorrect assumption, resulting in a confusion of all the characters and their unique dialects. Lewis abruptly halted and exclaimed, "Hey! Wait a minute!" in his natural voice. He regained his composure and resumed portraying each character with its appropriate dialect.[211]

Lewis traveled to Hollywood in 1943 to collaborate with Harold Peary on a film. From 1945 to 1971, he appeared in a little over thirty films, both credited and uncredited.[212] He began his television career in the 1950s by portraying Mr. Mack, the host of the ABC children's series *Sandy Strong* (1952). He was featured in a diverse selection of programs, mostly

---

[208] Dickson, Terry. "Forrest Lewis."
[209] Dickson, Terry. "Forrest Lewis."
[210] Dickson, Terry. "Forrest Lewis."
[211] Dickson, Terry. "Forrest Lewis."
[212] "Forrest Lewis." Wikipedia, Wikimedia Foundation, 24 June 2024.

Westerns, including *My Friend Flicka*, *The Man from Blackhawk*, *Riverboat*, *Colt .45*, and *Mackenzie's Raiders*. He also appeared on *The People's Choice*, *Going My Way*, *Harrigan and Son*, *Ichabod and Me*, *The Andy Griffith Show*, and *The Real McCoys*. [213]

Lewis married radio actress Elsa Grace Cross in Knightstown on August 23, 1917. Their union produced a son, Forrest Gallion Lewis. Forrest Lewis passed away in Burbank, California, on June 2, 1977.[214]

---

[213] Dickson, Terry. "Forrest Lewis."
[214] Thurgood, Lowell. "Forrest Lewis (1899-1977) - Find a Grave Memorial." Find a Grave, www.findagrave.com/memorial/100622920/forrest-lewis. Accessed 10 Nov. 2024.

xxxii. Arthur Q. Bryan. Circa 1955. Public domain.

Arthur Q. Bryan

Although Arthur Q. Bryan lent his voice to the iconic character Elmer Fudd in the Warner Bros. *Looney Tunes/Merrie Melodies* series for nineteen years, his career included much more than simply being Bugs Bunny's nemesis for generations of youngsters growing up between 1940 and 1959. Arthur Quirk Bryan, a native of Brooklyn, was a talented concert singer who showcased his vocal abilities in choirs across New York City.[215]

Even though he was working as an insurance clerk for the Mutual Life Insurance Company in 1918, his true ambition was to become a concert singer. Arthur got that opportunity during his radio debut in June 1926 at station WGBS in New York. Two years later, he was working as a tenor soloist at station WEAF. In addition, he had the chance to perform alongside the Seiberling Singers and the Jeddo Highlanders. In 1929, Arthur started working as an announcer for WOR in New Jersey. One of the programs he announced was the children's radio show *Uncle Don*.[216]

Bryan departed from WOR in 1931 and found employment at WCAU in Philadelphia as a writer/performer. He remained on the East Coast, moving between various stations, until 1936. At that point, he made the decision to relocate to Hollywood and pursue a career as a scenario writer for Paramount Pictures. This foray into screenwriting did not pan out, and Bryan found himself at KFWB, a local radio station owned by Warner

---

[215] Baxter, Devon. "Radio Round-up: Arthur Q. Bryan." RADIO ROUND-UP: Arthur Q. Bryan, 20 Sept. 2017.
[216] Baxter, Devon. "Radio Round-up: Arthur Q. Bryan."

Bros. He appeared on a show called *The Grouch Club*, alongside "grouchmaster" Jack Lescoulie, which was first aired around 1938.[217]

The Grouch Club was a talk show where the host, Jack Lescoulie, would listen to individuals who wanted to complain about any problem in their life. Bryan had a recurring role on the show as "The Little Man." His character's speech had a distinct characteristic where he couldn't pronounce certain sounds, often replacing "L" and "R" with "W." This unique trait was evident in many of his roles in animation and radio.[218]

Warner's animators and directors frequently visited KFWB, which was situated a few buildings away from the animation department on Sunset Boulevard.[219] Tex Avery, the mastermind behind beloved animated characters like Bugs Bunny, Daffy Duck, and Porky Pig, was captivated by Bryan's performance. He utilized Bryan for the character of Dangerous Dan McFoo in 1939. In this animated film, the character addresses the audience with the words, "Hewwo, ev-webody!"[220]

Bryan, who typically portrayed supporting characters on radio, was the star of a brief summer replacement series titled *Major Hoople* in 1942. He was chosen to portray Cousin Octavia's secretary/assistant, Lucius Llewellyn (with an Elmer Fudd voice), on *The Great Gildersleeve* during that fall. He performed various roles prior to portraying Floyd Munson, the barber, a character initially portrayed by Mel Blanc. His impressive work on the series caught the attention of writers Don Quinn and Phil Leslie, who decided to bring him on board the cast of their main show,

---

[217] Baxter, Devon. "Radio Round-up: Arthur Q. Bryan."
[218] "The Grouch Club." Wikipedia, Wikimedia Foundation, 2 Sept. 2022.
[219] Baxter, Devon. "Radio Round-up: Arthur Q. Bryan."
[220] "Tex Avery." Wikipedia, Wikimedia Foundation, 9 June 2024.

Fibber McGee and Molly, in 1943.[221] Bryan depicted Doc Gamble as a new rival for McGee after his previous neighbor, Throckmorton P. Gildersleeve, left to host his own show.[222]

Fibber and Dr. George Gamble, the local physician and surgeon, maintained a long-standing friendship and rivalry. The two frequently devised inventive remarks to disparage each other's excessive weight. Gale Gordon portrayed the town doctor in numerous episodes prior to Bryan joining the cast.[223]

During the second season of *The Great Gildersleeve*, pharmacist Richard Q. Peavey and barber Floyd Munson (Mel Blanc for the first year, Arthur Q. Bryan from December 1942 onward) joined Gildersleeve's circle of acquaintances. Floyd Munson was a marvelous prankster. He told Commissioner Gildersleeve that the only way to increase the profit of the water company was to dilute the water.

Munson's barbershop was located right across the street from Peavey's pharmacy. Although Floyd had only been married once, he always referred to his wife, Lovey, as "my present wife." He delighted in repeating old jokes. Upon assuming the role of Summerfield's water commissioner, Gildersleeve was affectionately dubbed "the Commish" by Floyd, and he referred to Mr. Peavey as "the Peave." Floyd was notorious for being a gossip, and Gildersleeve once said, "Sharing a secret with Floyd is the same as placing a full-page ad in the newspaper."

In the room above the barber shop, where Floyd presided at the piano, the musical aggregation known as the Jolly Boys (or "musical aggravation"

---

[221] "Arthur Q. Bryan." Wikipedia, Wikimedia Foundation, 27 May 2024.
[222] Baxter, Devon. "Radio Round-up: Arthur Q. Bryan."
[223] "Fibber McGee and Molly." Creative Serendipity Memories, 13 Nov. 2014.

as Floyd referred to it) convened and rehearsed. It made sense, given that they focused on barbershop quartet melodies.[224]

Always eager to take part in a diverse range of radio programs, Bryan traveled to New York regularly. In 1947, he made a brief appearance on *The Milton Berle Show* on the East Coast; however, he did not join the regular cast. Bryan also made frequent appearances in various episodes of *Screen Directors Playhouse* and *Lux Radio Theatre* throughout the 1940s. His performances on these programs showcased a wider range of acting skills compared to his comedy and variety shows.[225] Bryan appeared in numerous crime dramas and detective programs during the mid-1940s and early 1950s, such as *Richard Diamond, Private Detective* (1949-53), *The Man from Homicide* (1950-51), *Jeff Regan, Investigator* (1948-50), and *Adventures of Phillip Marlowe* (1947-58), featuring actor Dick Powell. He briefly assumed the role of Lieutenant Walt Levinson from Ed Begley in *Richard Diamond*.[226]

During the 1950s, Bryan had a full schedule with his vocal performances in radio and animated cartoons. In addition, he made appearances on television, serving as a panelist on the early TV quiz show *Quizzing the News* (1948-49). He appeared in various productions, mostly in small roles that lasted only one episode. One example is his appearance in the early television comedy, *Beulah*. In 1955, he secured a minor television role as the handyman Mr. Boggs in the short-lived CBS sitcom *Professional Father*. On *The Halls of Ivy*, Bryan portrayed Professor

---

[224] Stumpf, Charles, and Ben Ohmart. The Great Gildersleeve.
[225] Baxter, Devon. "Radio Round-up: Arthur Q. Bryan."
[226] Baxter, Devon. "Radio Round-up: Arthur Q. Bryan."

Warren, the head of the college's history department, a role he also held on the radio program of the same name.

In a twist of fate, on September 17, 1956, Bryan found himself battling acute gastritis just moments before the scheduled airing of an episode of *Producers' Showcase* titled "The Lord Don't Play Favorites." The timing couldn't have been worse, as Bryan was in the midst of rehearsing for the show when he was struck with this debilitating condition. Staging director Bretaigne Windust stepped in to take over from Bryan when the program aired.[227]

He continued to play his most iconic radio character Floyd Munson on *The Great Gildersleeve* until 1955 and retired his role of Doc Gamble on *Fibber McGee and Molly* two years later. His final voice recording for Warner Bros. took place on January 2, 1959, for Friz Freleng's "Person to Bunny" (1960), where he portrayed the character Elmer Fudd. Several months later, in November, Bryan tragically passed away from a heart attack at the age of sixty. Hal Smith took over providing Elmer Fudd's voice the following year.[228]

---

[227] "Arthur Q. Bryan." Wikipedia.
[228] Baxter, Devon. "Radio Round-up: Arthur Q. Bryan."

xxxiii. Shirley Mitchell. Circa 1943. Public domain.

Shirley Mitchell

Shirley Mitchell was a talented individual who made a name for herself in the world of American radio, film, and television. She gained recognition for her notable radio portrayal of the captivating Southern Belle Leila Ransom on *The Great Gildersleeve* program.

Leila, who was described by Mr. Peavey as a "well-preserved Southern lady," moved into the neighboring house previously occupied by the Dobsons in the autumn of 1942. Leila's character's introduction into the story line provided ample opportunities for Gildersleeve to express his romantic sentiments through song. The widow Ransom delighted in playing the piano and frequently shared with her neighbor her deep affection for the song "Speak to Me of Love." She would even convince "Thrawkmawtinnnn" to serenade her with it on multiple occasions. Essentially, the dynamic between the flirtatious widow and her overweight suitor transformed into a lighthearted chase. She teased him by frequently mentioning her past romantic partners, such as Lightfoot Duprez, who worked in the cotton industry, and her late husband Beauregard Ransom, a respected southern gentleman.[229]

Gildersleeve became infatuated with Leila, leading to their inevitable engagement. Upon hearing the news of their impending nuptials, Marjorie organized a wedding shower to celebrate the couple. The wedding was scheduled to take place on June 6, 1943, with Judge Hooker serving as the best man.[230] Yet, it seemed that the Southern Belle had failed to

---

[229] Stumpf, Charles, and Ben Ohmart. "The Great Gildersleeve."
[230] Stumpf, Charles, and Ben Ohmart. "The Great Gildersleeve."

consider the possibility that Beauregard might still be alive. Right as the minister was on the verge of declaring Throckmorton and Leila as husband and wife, Beauregard made a dramatic entrance, causing the wedding to come to an abrupt halt. Leila set off from Summerfield alongside Beauregard. Devastated, Gildersleeve discovered himself left alone within the confines of the church.[231] Shortly afterwards, news arrived from Savannah that Leila had indeed become a widow. Beauregard had tragically lost his life due to a fatal kick from a mule. The widow quickly returned to Summerfield, where the old romance was reignited.

Nevertheless, the romance between Leila and Gildersleeve was far from simple. The Southern Belle often found herself captivated by the charm of other handsome gentlemen, like Dr. Arthur Hargreve. She would frequently disappear from Summerfield for long stretches of time, only to unexpectedly return just as Gildersleeve was starting to develop feelings for someone new.[232]

Mitchell was born in Toledo, Ohio on November 4, 1919, to Sam Mitchell, a dry cleaner, and his wife, Mary Ann Daniels. Shirley's passion for the stage was ignited as a child. She captivated the entire neighborhood with her remarkable imitations of well-known locals, organizing her friends into meticulously choreographed performances in barns, attics, and garages. Her father's dry-cleaning business was successful, allowing her the opportunity to attend college. She pursued her passion for drama at the University of Michigan and went on to

---

[231] Stumpf, Charles, and Ben Ohmart. "The Great Gildersleeve."
[232] Stumpf, Charles, and Ben Ohmart. "The Great Gildersleeve."

perform with theater groups in various locations, from Cleveland to Massachusetts.[233]

Stock company life was an education in and of itself for Shirley, but there was never much money in it. Shirley knew she wanted something more consistent, and she discovered it in radio. By the late 1930s, the major primetime shows had left the Midwest for Hollywood, but Chicago remained a significant network hub for dramatic features. After moving to Chicago, Mitchell appeared in the network broadcast of *The First Nighter* and performed small roles in various soap operas, including *The Story of Mary Marlin* and *The Road of Life*.[234]

Before long, she secured a part on a show called *Hap Hazard*, featuring the renowned Ransom Sherman, a former Chicago radio comic. Because of his assortment of quirky personas, Sherman was always a favorite among Midwest radio listeners. However, regardless of his multiple attempts, none of his formats managed to strike a chord with the national audiences. Nevertheless, his afternoon variety show *Club Matinee* quickly gained a loyal following. Once he arrived in Hollywood, he discovered himself playing supporting roles alongside the incredibly talented cast of *Fibber McGee and Molly*. In 1941, he persuaded the sponsor, Johnson's Wax, to grant him the summer replacement spot and, recalling Mitchell's work in Chicago, he extended an invitation for her to relocate to the west and join his cast.[235]

---

[233] McLeod, Elizabeth. "'Why, Thrawkmawtinnnnnnnn...' The Radio Life of Shirley Mitchell." Radio Classics, 4 Nov. 2016.
[234] "Shirley Mitchell Famous Death." Khoolood, 6 Nov. 2014.
[235] McLeod, Elizabeth.

Just like many of Sherman's other formats, the summer replacement failed to secure a sponsor, preventing it from becoming a permanent part of the broadcast schedule. Shirley Mitchell found herself facing a lack of demand for her talents, which led her to consider a potential career change in Toledo. As time went on, however, the calls began to pour in. In September of 1941, she secured a role in a new Sunday-afternoon situation comedy that had recently spun-off from *Fibber McGee and Molly*, with Harold Peary taking the lead role. The script featured a character named Dorabelle, a friend of Gildersleeve's niece, who came for a visit and ended up flirting with Gildersleeve. Mitchell depicted the role with a rich, languid Southern accent. There was instant chemistry between Mitchell and Peary. Impressed with the young actress's performance, producer Cecil Underwood took note of her name.[236]

As 1941 concluded and 1942 commenced, Shirley Mitchell found other work. Her role in *The Sealtest Village Store* was opposite Joan Davis and Jack Haley. Additionally, she played the role of Louella in *The Life of Riley*.[237] Shirley began playing supporting roles on Rudy Vallee's show, and in the summer of 1942, she received a call from Cecil Underwood. John Whedon, a new writer, had been recruited to take over producing the scripts for *The Great Gildersleeve*. He came up with a semi-serialized format that gave Gildersleeve the opportunity to have a recurring love interest. Mitchell's portrayal of Dorabelle left a lasting impact on Underwood and Whedon, inspiring them to craft a new character who would take Gildersleeve on a truly unforgettable journey.

---

[236] McLeod, Elizabeth.
[237] "Shirley Mitchell Famous Death."

Early in Gildersleeve's second season, the flirty widow Leila Ransom moved into the neighborhood, and the fun began. Whedon created an on-again, off-again plot that kept viewers guessing until the finale. Listeners were relieved to see Gildersleeve slip out from Leila's clutches in the season's last episode, as the wedding fell through at the last minute. But everyone knew she'd be back to try again.[238]

And she was. Shirley Mitchell portrayed the character of Leila Ransom for a significant portion of the following decade, making multiple departures and returns. She portrayed Leila as a character who embodied a unique blend of charm and cunning. Her demeanor exuded warmth and kindness, but beneath the surface, there was a hidden fierceness. Leila emerged as the quintessential character that listeners couldn't help but despise. Mitchell found this somewhat unsettling, but even before her first season with Gildersleeve was over she had discovered another role that was much more appealing.[239]

She joined the *Fibber McGee and Molly* cast in December of 1942. The war had caused chaos for that program, which was known for its strong Tuesday night ratings. Actor Bill Thompson, recognized for his memorable voice work on the show, joined the Navy, while actor Gale Gordon, who played important roles, joined the Coast Guard. Producer Underwood and writer Don Quinn quickly filled the vacancies, with Mitchell being an early selection. Mitchell took on supporting roles for several months, and in October 1943, she became a regular as Alice Darling, a bright and optimistic young war worker who rented a room at 79 Wistful Vista. Portrayed by Mitchell in her authentic voice, Alice was

---

[238] McLeod, Elizabeth.
[239] McLeod, Elizabeth.

the complete opposite of Leila in nearly every aspect—kind, modest, and maybe a little scatterbrained. However, she possessed Leila's strong desire for male companionship.[240]

Alice vanished following the war, while Leila continued to make regular appearances on postwar radio, and Shirley Mitchell's radio career flourished. She married Dr. Julian Frieden, a physician from Los Angeles, on November 26, 1946. Despite her busy schedule, she became a mother to a son named Scott and a daughter named Brooke.

Mitchell and Frieden ended their marriage in August 1974. In 1992, Shirley married songwriter Jay Livingston, known for his collaborations with Ray Evans on several Academy Award-winning songs. Some of these notable songs include "Mona Lisa" performed by Nat King Cole, "Que Sera, Sera" by Doris Day, and "Buttons and Bows" by Bob Hope. The couple remained married until his death in 2001.[241]

Shirley seamlessly made her way into the world of television during the early 1950s. During her time on the radio show *My Favorite Husband*, she formed a strong bond with Lucille Ball, forging a close friendship. Mitchell joined the beloved ensemble of Lucille Ball's *I Love Lucy* in the 1953-54 season. Within this program, she took on the role of Marion Strong, a dear companion to Lucy Ricardo, recognized for her unique and contagious laughter. In one episode, Lucy tells Mitchell "Marion, stop cackling. I've been waiting ten years for you to lay that egg!"[242]

---

[240] McLeod, Elizabeth.
[241] Barnes, Mike. "'I Love Lucy' Actress Shirley Mitchell Dies at 94." The Hollywood Reporter, The Hollywood Reporter, 13 Nov. 2013.
[242] Barnes, Mike. "'I Love Lucy' Actress Shirley Mitchell Dies at 94."

Mitchell was highly sought after as a television actress during the 1950s and 60s. She has an impressive TV résumé that includes a wide range of shows such as *Bachelor Father, Please Don't Eat the Daisies, Petticoat Junction, Pete and Gladys, The Jack Benny Program, The Beverly Hillbillies, Make Room for Daddy, Perry Mason, The Loretta Young Show, The Mothers-in-Law, The Doris Day Show, Green Acres, The Odd Couple, Chico and the Man, Three's Company, Trapper John, M.D., Dallas*, and *The Fresh Prince of Bel-Air.*

Mitchell also appeared on the big screen in such films as *Jamboree* (1944), *Desk Set* (1957), *Big Business* (1988), and *The War of the Roses* (1989).[243]

Shirley resumed her career in radio acting in the late 1970s, working with producer Elliott Lewis on the *Sears Radio Theatre*. She was thrilled to have the opportunity to collaborate with her former colleagues once again.

She quickly gained popularity in the old-time radio convention circuit, delighting audiences with her performances as Leila Ransom alongside Willard Waterman, in a variety of on-stage re-creations. Additionally, she explored the realm of animation voice work lending her voice to the character Laurie Holiday on the Hanna-Barbera cartoon series *The Roman Holidays*.[244]

Sadly, on November 11, 2013, Mitchell passed away due to heart failure. She was ninety-four years old.[245]

---

[243] "Shirley Mitchell Famous Death.".
[244] Barnes, Mike.
[245] "Shirley Mitchell Famous Death."

xxxiv. Gildersleeve with Leila and Eve. Circa 1940s. Public domain.

Bea Benaderet

A new woman came into Throckmorton's life during one of Leila Ransom's frequent absences from Summerfield. Eve Goodwin, the principal of Leroy's school, paid a visit to the house to discuss the boy's less-than-satisfactory academic performance. Her genuine interest captivated Throckmorton, who found himself drawn to her at once.

Unlike Leila, Eve had no interest in glamour or frivolity. Quite the contrary, she exuded eloquence, maintained a calm demeanor, and carried herself with refinement. Although she valued his kind words, she always remained genuine and direct, never purposely leading him on. Everything was going well until Leila came back to town unexpectedly. She was instantly overcome with jealousy upon seeing Miss Goodwin and reverted back to her seductive ways. Throckmorton was drawn in two different directions at the same time.

During his campaign for Mayor of Summerfield, Gildersleeve misunderstood a passing remark from Eve. She mentioned that she would marry him if he won the election. He briefly believed that she was being sincere. However, her mother, who was known for being challenging, arrived for a visit. Despite Gildersleeve's sincere efforts to win her over, she remained unresponsive to his persistent flattery and actively created barriers to their blossoming relationship.

Later on, Eve was informed by her brother Fred that he had enlisted in the Seabees, the United States Naval Construction Battalions. He also mentioned that their mother would be staying in Summerfield for the duration of the war. Throckmorton and Eve had a long chat and decided not to marry but remained close friends.[246]

Beatrice Benaderet, a New York City native who grew up in San Francisco, began her career in Bay Area theater and radio before making her way to Hollywood. There, she embarked on a remarkable career that spanned over three decades. During the golden age of radio, she found her passion in voice-over work. She was a regular guest on a variety of programs, working alongside famous comedians of the era such as Jack Benny, Burns and Allen, and Lucille Ball. With her exceptional command of dialect and ability to bring characters to life, she became the leading voice for female characters in Warner Bros.' animated cartoons from the early 1940s to the mid-1950s.

In 1926, Benaderet became a member of the staff at San Francisco radio station KFRC. During her time there, she took on a variety of responsibilities, including acting, singing, writing, and producing.

Bea moved to Hollywood in 1936 and joined radio station KHJ. She made her network radio debut alongside Orson Welles with his Mercury Theatre repertory company, which was featured on *The Campbell Playhouse*. The following year, she got her big break on *The Jack Benny Program*. Her role as Gertrude Gearshift, a sharp-tongued telephone operator who engaged in gossip about Jack Benny alongside her colleague Mabel Flapsaddle (Sara Berner), marked a pivotal moment in her professional career. Intended as a one-time appearance, the pair ended up becoming regulars starting in the 1945–46 season.

---

[246] Stumpf, Charles, and Ben Ohmart. "The Great Gildersleeve."

She played several recurring roles throughout her career, including Blanche Morton on *The George Burns and Gracie Allen Show*, Millicent Carstairs on *Fibber McGee and Molly*, maid Gloria on *The Adventures of Ozzie and Harriet,* and Iris Atterbury on *My Favorite Husband*, alongside Gale Gordon. Benaderet provided voice work for several minor roles before becoming a regular cast member, portraying Iris, the neighbor and close companion of Lucille Ball's character, Liz Cooper. The 1950 CBS program *Granby's Green Acres* was a radio show that many considered to be a spinoff of *My Favorite Husband*. The show brought together the talented duo Gale Gordon and Bea Benaderet, who portrayed a married couple that abandoned urban living to embark on a farming career. Regrettably, the show had a brief run, consisting of just eight episodes.

Benaderet became a well-known presence on television in situation comedies afterwards. She appeared on *The George Burns and Gracie Allen Show* from 1950 to 1958, receiving two Emmy Award nominations for Best Supporting Actress. During the 1960s, she held regular roles in four television series until her passing in 1968 due to lung cancer. These series included popular shows such as *The Beverly Hillbillies, The Flintstones,* and her most recognized role as Kate Bradley in *Petticoat Junction*.[247]

---

[247] "Bea Benaderet." Wikipedia, Wikimedia Foundation, 19 July 2024.

xxxv. Cathy Lewis. Public domain.

Cathy Lewis

In *The Great Gildersleeve*, Nurse Katherine Milford and Principal Irene Henshaw, two of Throckmorton's love interests, were brought to life by the talented American actress Cathy Lewis, known for her work in radio, film, and television. Catherine Lee Lewis, born in Spokane, Washington on December 27, 1916, is widely recognized for her extensive work in radio, as well as her notable contributions to film and television in the later years of her career.

As per Ronald W. Lackmann's *The Encyclopedia of American Radio: An A-Z Guide to Radio from Jack Benny to Howard Stern* (1999), Lewis relocated from Spokane, Washington to Chicago and secured a job on radio on *The First Nighter* program. According to other sources, it is said that she initially aspired to pursue a career in singing.[248] In 1936, Lewis embarked on a new chapter of her life in Hollywood. It was there that she had the opportunity to showcase her singing talents alongside Kay Kyser's orchestra. At the same time, she honed her acting skills through an apprenticeship at the prestigious Pasadena Playhouse.[249]

Afterwards, she found work in West Coast radio, where she made appearances on popular programs like *Lights Out*, *The Lux Radio Theatre*, *Theatre of Romance*, *Michael Shayne Private Detective*, *The Philip Morris Playhouse*, and *The Adventures of Sam Spade*. Cathy was a member of the renowned repertory company known as "Whistler's Children," who were often featured on the popular radio mystery show,

---

[248] "Cathy Lewis." Wikipedia, Wikimedia Foundation, 10 Feb. 2024.
[249] Shreve, Ivan G. "Happy Birthday, Cathy Lewis!" Radio Classics, 27 Dec. 2021.

The Whistler. She became a regular on *Suspense*, starring alongside Robert Taylor in the memorable episode "The House in Cypress Canyon," and sharing the stage with Cary Grant in the renowned broadcast "On a Country Road."[250]

Cathy Lewis had plenty of experience with radio comedy as well. She had the privilege of working on programs featuring iconic performers like Rudy Vallee, Eddie Bracken, and Dennis Day.[251] She would be best known as the practical and witty secretary Jane Stacy, who was the roommate of the absent-minded Irma Peterson, played by Marie Wilson, in the popular radio and television comedy *My Friend Irma*, which aired from 1947 to 1954.[252] According to legend, Cathy, in a rush for yet another appointment, started to feel a bit restless during her *My Friend Irma* audition. It was then that writer Cy Howard, intrigued by the irritated quality in her voice, decided to offer her the role.[253] Cathy was honored for her contributions as Jane Stacy, receiving the prestigious Ideal Secretary Award from the Executive Secretaries Club in 1948. She portrayed the character of Jane Stacy until 1953, with a brief hiatus due to exhaustion.[254] Lewis was juggling her role in *My Friend Irma* with her appearances as Nurse Kathryn Milford on *The Great Gildersleeve*.[255]

Lewis met actor Elliott Lewis (who coincidentally shared the same surname) during their recording session at The Woodbury Playhouse on November 6, 1940. On April 30, 1943, during Elliott's leave from the Army, they tied the knot at Chapman Park Hotel in Los Angeles. Elliott's

---

[250] Shreve, Ivan G. "Happy Birthday, Cathy Lewis!"
[251] Shreve, Ivan G. "Happy Birthday, Cathy Lewis!"
[252] "Cathy Lewis." Wikipedia.
[253] Shreve, Ivan G. "Happy Birthday, Cathy Lewis!"
[254] "Cathy Lewis." Wikipedia.
[255] Shreve, Ivan G. "Happy Birthday, Cathy Lewis!"

uncle Eddie Raiden was selected as the best man. Collaboratively, the couple dedicated their efforts to timeless radio masterpieces like *The Voyage of the Scarlet Queen* and *Suspense*. They brought in a combined annual income of $90,000 and were known as "Mr. and Mrs. Radio."[256]

The Lewises were part of the esteemed group of performers known as "Hollywood's Radio Row," making frequent appearances on popular shows. One of their notable collaborations was the creation of the anthology series *On Stage*. They also worked together on an episode of *Suspense* called "The Thirteenth Sound," which was broadcasted in 1947, and an episode of *Twelve Players* titled "Checkerboard," which aired in 1948.

On their fourteenth wedding anniversary, Cathy and Elliot decided to part ways. Cathy took the step of filing for divorce, citing mental cruelty as the reason. The divorce was finalized on April 16, 1958, marking the end of their era as the iconic "Mr. and Mrs. Radio." In the same year, Cathy had a supporting role in the film *The Party Crashers*.

The majority of Cathy's film work during the 1940s consisted of small, uncredited roles. She portrayed her famous character from *My Friend Irma* on television during the show's first two seasons. However, due to exhaustion and a growing dissatisfaction with the role, she decided to walk away from the show in 1953. In 1959, she played a leading role in the short-lived television series *Fibber McGee and Molly*, alongside Bob Sweeney as Fibber.[257]

---

[256] "Cathy Lewis." Wikipedia.
[257] "Cathy Lewis." Wikipedia.

Her final appearance on screen occurred in a 1965 episode of the comedy western, *F-Troop*. However, she had another remarkable contribution to make: providing her voice for Jade, a fearless female spy/adventurer who appeared in two episodes of the original *Jonny Quest* animated series. On November 20, 1968, Cathy Lewis sadly lost her battle with breast cancer at the age of fifty-one. For a considerable portion of her life—thirty-five long years—she poured her heart and soul into the captivating world of show business. [258]

---

[258] "Cathy Lewis." Wikipedia.

xxxvi. Gale Gordon as Rumson Bullard. Public domain.

xxxvii. Gale Gordon and Bea Benaderet Granby's Green Acres 1950. Public domain.

Gale Gordon

Gale Gordon was a highly respected actor in the radio industry during the late 1940s, renowned for his talent in delivering comedic moments with a perfectly timed temper explosion. He made frequent appearances on *The Great Gildersleeve*, *The Halls of Ivy*, *My Favorite Husband*, *The Penny Singleton Show*, and *Junior Miss*. He was the first actor to portray the iconic character of Flash Gordon in the 1935 radio serial *The Amazing Interplanetary Adventures of Flash Gordon*.[259]

Charles Thomas Aldrich Jr., later known as Gale Gordon, was born in New York City on February 2, 1906. His parents were vaudevillian Charles Thomas Aldrich and English actress Gloria Gordon. Gale Gordon made his debut on radio at station KFWB in Los Angeles in 1926. Throughout the next decade, he primarily took on supporting roles in radio shows such as *Tarzan*, *Gangbusters*, and *Death Valley Days*. Gordon's initial foray into comedy on radio occurred in 1939 when he made his debut on *The Joe E. Brown Show*. However, it wasn't until 1941, when he joined the cast of *Fibber McGee & Molly*, that he truly found a role that he could sink his teeth into. His recurring roles of Mayor La Trivia and Foggy Williams on *Fibber McGee and Molly* paved the way for his portrayal of Rumson Bullard on the popular spinoff, *The Great Gildersleeve*.[260]

Foggy Williams was the local weatherman and next-door neighbor known for his inventive tales, willingness to lend tools to Fibber, and humorously

---

[259] "Gale Gordon." Radio Hall Of Fame.
[260] "Gale Gordon." Radio Hall Of Fame.

accepting responsibility for the current weather conditions. He often signed off with his signature line, "Good day... probably."[261] Mayor La Trivia was the mayor of Wistful Vista, a character inspired by the mayor of New York, Fiorello La Guardia. In later episodes, Fibber sometimes referred to the mayor as "Homer," leaving us unsure if this was his real first name or simply another one of the show's mysterious naming jokes, similar to The Old Timer calling Fibber "Johnny." The McGees' usual routine with La Trivia involved Fibber and Molly misunderstanding a figure of speech, similar to Abbott & Costello's famous Who's on First? routine. La Trivia would gradually transition from attempting calm explanations to frustrated outbursts, in Gale Gordon's iconic slow-burn style. Occasionally, it becomes clear from Fibber and Molly's conversation after he departed that they were deliberately taunting him.[262]

In the spring of 1945, Rumson Bullard, a wealthy and snobbish individual, moved to Summerfield and settled into a posh residence in Gildersleeve's neighborhood. The new neighbor appeared to have an inflated sense of self-importance, clearly believing himself to be superior to others. Bullard regarded everyone, particularly Gildersleeve, with an air of superiority. Gildersleeve disliked his arrogant behavior, and the two soon became enemies.

Bullard had two sons: Marshall, who was a teenager, and Craig, who was closer in age to Leroy. Both of them lacked the class consciousness displayed by their arrogant father. Marshall and Marjorie developed a mutual attraction and subsequently went on a few dates. When it seemed

---

[261] "Fibber McGee and Molly." Creative Serendipity Memories.
[262] "Fibber McGee and Molly." Creative Serendipity Memories.

that a serious relationship was forming, there were significant objections from both families.

Regrettably, due to conflicting rehearsal schedules, Gordon had to relinquish the role. Jim Backus was appointed as his replacement.[263]

Gordon's most famous role is that of the strict principal on *Our Miss Brooks*, which he accepted in 1948. Osgood Conklin was a character that listeners couldn't help but despise, whether he was mocking student Walter Denton with his dry wit or unleashing one of his infamous fits of anger on teacher Connie Brooks. Gordon carried over the role to television when the show transitioned in 1952.[264]

He also portrayed the character of John Granby, a former city man who is ineptly pursuing his ambition of living on a farm, in the 1950 radio series *Granby's Green Acres*, which served as the foundation for the 1960s television series *Green Acres*. In the interim, Gordon appeared as Rudolph Atterbury in *My Favorite Husband*, a predecessor to *I Love Lucy* starring Lucille Ball.[265]

Gordon and Ball previously collaborated on *The Wonder Show*, which starred Jack Haley, from 1938 to 1939. The two enjoyed a long friendship as well as a professional partnership. Gordon also had a regular role as Mr. Scott, the imaginary Rexall Drugs sponsor representative, on another radio hit, *The Phil Harris-Alice Faye Show*, for as long as Rexall sponsored the program. When the sponsor shifted to RCA, the character simply changed jobs.[266]

---

[263] Stumpf, Charles, and Ben Ohmart. "The Great Gildersleeve."
[264] "Gale Gordon." Radio Hall Of Fame.
[265] "Gale Gordon." Radio Hall Of Fame.
[266] "Gale Gordon." Radio Hall Of Fame.

Gordon passed away from lung cancer on June 30, 1995, at the Redwood Terrace Health Center in Escondido, California, at the age of eighty-nine. His wife, Virginia Curley, had passed away in the same facility just a month prior. The couple had no children. Gordon was posthumously inducted into the Radio Hall of Fame in 1999. Additionally, he is honored with a star on the Hollywood Walk of Fame at 6340 Hollywood Boulevard in recognition of his contributions to radio.[267]

---

[267] "Gale Gordon." Wikipedia, Wikimedia Foundation, 7 June 2024.

xxxviii. Jim Backus and Jone Allison performing on Casey's Girl Friday. Circa 1943. Public domain.

xxxix. Jim Backus performing for the NBC Blue Network. Circa 1940s. Public domain.

Jim Backus

Prior to gaining fame as Thurston Howell III, the affluent and arrogant character from the popular TV series *Gilligan's Island*, Jim Backus had already made a name for himself in radio through his recurring role on *The Alan Young Show*. With his portrayal of the character Hubert Updike III, he breathed life into a hilariously pompous and affluent persona. Armed with his limited understanding of the world, Updike made a solemn promise to retaliate against a disrespectful comment by using a bottle of "domestic champagne" to cleanse the offender's mouth. Therefore, it was fitting for Jim to assume the role of Gildersleeve's pompous neighbor Rumson Bullard, filling in for Gale Gordon, in the later episodes of *The Great Gildersleeve*.[268]

Bakus, a graduate of the American Academy of Dramatic Arts in New York in 1933, was widely acclaimed throughout his career in the entertainment industry for his exceptional talent as a comedic character actor. Despite completing a brief apprenticeship at various stock companies after graduation, the life of a struggling actor during the Great Depression was incredibly challenging. He explained, "I decided to try radio as a source of livelihood because I like to eat regularly."[269] While simultaneously auditioning for Broadway acting roles, he began working as a freelance actor on New York's Radio Row.

Jim Backus was born in Bratenahl, a prestigious neighborhood in Cleveland, Ohio, in 1913. His father, a mechanical engineer, found it

---

[268] "Jim Backus Collection." Old Time Radio, www.otrcat.com.
[269] "Jim Backus Collection." Old Time Radio.

difficult to comprehend his son's deep love for the art of acting. It is possible that Jim's aspirations were influenced by his kindergarten teacher, Ms. Margaret Hamilton, who later portrayed the Wicked Witch of the West in MGM's *The Wizard of Oz* (1939). Jim was far from thrilled when his father decided to send him off to the Kentucky Military Institute to become a cadet. With a mischievous glint in his eye, he decided to make a grand entrance by galloping on a horse right through the cadet mess hall in the middle of lunch. Naturally, he was expelled.[270]

Backus moved to Hollywood to pursue a career in the film industry. He costarred with Lucille Ball and his buddy Victor Mature, whom he had met at the Kentucky Military Institute, in his first recognized motion picture performance in 1949, *Easy Living*. Meanwhile, he stumbled upon numerous job prospects in the bustling Los Angeles radio industry.[271] Jim was featured on a variety of programs throughout the 1940s, including *The Penny Singleton Show, The Aldrich Family, December Bride, Fibber McGee and Molly, The Halls of Ivy, The Life of Riley, Life with Luigi, Lum 'n' Abner, The Magnificent Montague, Mr. and Mrs. Blandings, My Favorite Husband, Our Miss Broo*ks, and *The Phil Harris & Alice Faye Show*. He portrayed an affluent aviator named Dexter Hayes in the radio series *Society Girl*, a character that would essentially serve as his trademark in his diverse radio roles.[272]

Given Backus' extensive radio experience, it was only natural for him to excel in voicing cartoon characters. The actor achieved great fame through a successful audition for a 1949 cartoon called *Ragtime Bear*.

---

[270] "Jim Backus Collection." Old Time Radio.
[271] "Jim Backus Collection." Old Time Radio.
[272] "Jim Backus Collection." Old Time Radio.

Thus began a string of appearances by Quincy Magoo, a character with impaired vision who frequently found himself in comical situations because of his stubborn refusal to see an eye doctor. Jim was the voice behind Magoo in over fifty short films until 1959. He then continued his work with a feature film and a TV series in 1960. Magoo was the subject of a popular animated series that aired during prime time in 1964-1965, and later had a revival on Saturday mornings in the 1970s. [273]

Jim Backus gained recognition on television for his role as Judge Bradley Stevens, the husband of Joan Davis' character, on the sitcom *I Married Joan*, which aired from 1952 to 1955. One of Joan's writers was Sherwood Schwartz, who had also written a significant portion of Hubert Updike's dialogue on *The Alan Young Show*. When Schwartz conceived the idea for *Gilligan's Island*, he drew inspiration from Jim when crafting the character of Thurston Howell III. Schwartz then asked Jim to take on the role, which he accepted. Jim had a successful three-season run as the beloved character on television, with Natalie Schafer playing his wife Lovey. He also reprised the role for three TV-movies that aired in 1979 and 1981, as well as two animated spin-offs: *The New Adventures of Gilligan* (1974-75) and *Gilligan's Planet* (1982).[274]

Jim was frequently sought after as a guest star on various popular television programs, ranging from *The Beverly Hillbillies* to *The Love Boat*. However, his acting career in the 1980s was hindered by Parkinson's disease. His final film credit was in 1984's *Prince Jack*, and he bid farewell to television with an Orville Redenbacher Popcorn commercial, where he reunited with his *Gilligan's Island* co-star, Natalie

---

[273] "Jim Backus Collection." Old Time Radio.
[274] Shreve, Ivan G. "Happy Birthday, Jim Backus!" Radio Spirits, 25 Feb. 2017.

Schafer. Jim passed away in 1989 from complications due to pneumonia. He was seventy-six.[275] He is commemorated with a star on the Hollywood Walk of Fame at 1735 Vine Street for his notable contributions to television.[276]

---

[275] Shreve, Ivan G. "Happy Birthday, Jim Backus!"
[276] "Jim Backus Collection." Old Time Radio.

Ken Christy

Ken Christy, known for his role as Police Chief Gates in *The Great Gildersleeve*, enjoyed a successful career in radio spanning almost three decades, starting in the early 1930s. He was a versatile artist who appeared on a variety of classic shows, including *The Alan Young Show, The Saint, Amos 'n' Andy, A Day in the Life of Dennis Day, Suspense, The Fifth Horseman, Gangbusters, Jack Armstrong the All-American Boy*, and *Little Orphan Annie*. He was typically featured as a law enforcement officer in a variety of radio and film productions. In 1950, Christy stated in an interview with the *Shamokin News-Dispatch*, "I'd give anything to stop making arrests and be the guy who commits the crime for once."[277]

Police Chief Gates was a member of the Summerfield social group known as the Jolly Boys, recognized for his distinctive phrase spoken in a calm, deep, and resonant voice: "Fellas! Fellas! Let's all be Jolly Boys," whenever the men engaged in some form of dispute.

He transitioned to television in 1949, landing a role in the anthology series *Arch Oboler Comedy Theatre*. Altogether, he appeared in twenty-three television programs, one of which was *I Love Lucy*. In his first appearance, he played Fred's close friend and private investigator. The gang suspected that he might be investigating the Johnsons, the new

---

[277] "Victoria: Top Performers Appear in 'No Way Out'." Shamokin News-Dispatch, Newspapers.com, 6 Oct. 1950.

neighbors, who they suspected of being involved in a scam selling fake oil wells.

Although often cast in supporting roles, Christy had an impressive body of work, having appeared in 144 films from 1940 to 1957. Some of the notable titles in his filmography include *Foreign Correspondent, Here Comes Mr. Jordan, Ball of Fire, The Glass Key, Hello, Frisco, Hello, Cheaper by the Dozen, Sunset Boulevard, My Sister Eileen,* and *Escape From San Quentin.*[278]

Robert Kenneth Christy, born in Greenville, Pennsylvania on November 23, 1894, was a veteran of World War I.[279]

He made his last on-screen appearance in a March 1962 episode of *Shannon*, featuring George Nader. Christy passed away on July 23, 1962 in Los Angeles. He was sixty-seven.[280]

---

[278] Davis, Linda. "Ken Christy (1894-1962) - Find a Grave Memorial." Find a Grave.
[279] Davis, Linda. "Ken Christy (1894-1962) - Find a Grave Memorial." Find a Grave.
[280] Davis, Linda. "Ken Christy (1894-1962) - Find a Grave Memorial." Find a Grave.

xl. Ken Christy who portrayed Police Chief Gates on The Great Gildersleeve. Circa 1953. Public domain.

xli. Katie Lee with Willard Waterman on The Great Gildersleeve. Circa 1948. Public domain.

Katie Lee

American folk singer, actress, writer, and environmental activist, Katie Lee, appeared as herself multiple times on *The Great Gildersleeve* in the early 1950s. After her arrival in California in 1948, she had many jobs performing on radio shows and eventually television, usually as a folk singer. After her first appearance on *The Great Gildersleeve* aired, her popularity led the producers to feature her in several episodes.[281]

In an interview Katie gave to Jim Stiles of the *Canyon Country Zephyr* in 2002, she claimed that she received over five hundred cards and letters from all over the United States, after the first episode aired. She went on to say that Willard Waterman felt threatened and "asked the writers not to be so generous with my character."[282]

Kathryn Louise Lee was born on October 23, 1919 in Aledo, Illinois. At the age of three months, her family relocated to Tucson, Arizona. Her father pursued a career as an architect and homebuilder, while her mother found her passion in the field of decorating. Katie was encouraged by her mother to learn the piano and she learned to hunt small game like rabbit and quail using a Remington shotgun under her father's guidance. Securing the lead role in a high school production titled *The Patsy* filled her with a deep sense of familiarity and comfort, as if the stage were an extension of her own home.[283]

---

[281] Rapaport, Diane. "Katie Lee and Great Gildersleeve." Drapaport's Blog, 2 Mar. 2015.
[282] Stiles, Jim. "Live! With Katie Lee." Canyon Country Zephyr, 2002.
[283] Sandomir, Richard. "Katie Lee, Folk Singer Who Fought to Protect a Canyon, Dies at 98." The New York Times, The New York Times, 10 Nov. 2017.

Upon completing her Bachelor of Fine Arts in Drama at the University of Arizona, she relocated to Hollywood to receive instruction from renowned folksingers Burl Ives and Josh White.[284] Her professional career began in 1948 as an actress in both stage and screen productions. She had small roles in films and made appearances on radio shows like *The Great Gildersleeve*, *Halls of Ivy*, and *The Railroad Hour* with Gordon McRae.[285]

During the 1950s, Katie changed her career path and became a well-known folk singer in popular cabarets such as the Hungry Eye in San Francisco, The Blue Angel in New York, and the Gate of Horn in Chicago. She was instrumental in organizing the Cabaret Concert Theatre, a popular folk music venue in Hollywood that attracted renowned artists such as Josh White, Burl Ives, and Carl Sandburg. She started her recording career in 1975 with a series of albums produced by Bud Freeman. In Novato, California, Katie recorded *Love's Little Sisters*, a compilation of folk songs about the early American women involved in the sex trade, at Mickey Hart's (from the Grateful Dead) studio.[286]

Lee eventually teamed up with notable conservationists like David Brower, the executive director of the Sierra Club, and writer Edward Abbey in their mission to stop the building of the towering Glen Canyon Dam in Northern Arizona. In 1963, the dam was successfully completed and opened. She became part of a passionate group of environmental advocates who have been tirelessly advocating for the restoration of the canyon. Her deep-seated frustration with the federal government,

---

[284] "Katie Lee (Singer)." Wikipedia, Wikimedia Foundation, 8 July 2024.
[285] Martin, Tom. "Katie Lee Remembered." Mountain Buzz, 5 Nov. 2017.
[286] Martin, Tom. "Katie Lee Remembered."

particularly the Bureau of Reclamation and their construction of the Glen Canyon Dam, became a driving force behind her musical pursuits and caught the eye of filmmakers. Her songs revolved around the enchanting tales of flowing rivers and the courageous boatmen who navigated them. With her protest songs, she passionately voiced her disapproval toward those responsible for dam construction. After the dam was constructed, she never went back to Glen Canyon.[287]

She wrote a total of five books, including a remarkable trilogy focused on Glen Canyon. In addition, she created a total of fourteen CDs and two DVDs. With her vast knowledge of the Southwest, she became a highly sought-after guest for TV shows and documentary films.[288]

According to available records, it appears Lee was married on three separate occasions. Her first marriage was to Charles Eld, a figure who is mentioned in her book *Sandstone Seduction*. She wrote that she "...went to work for the war effort at Davis Monthan Field, married a shavetail in '42, got pregnant, had a son, [and] got divorced in '45." This son is identified as Ronald Eld in the New York Times obituary from November 10, 2017. Charles was granted full custody of Ronald in 1950. In her journal from the 1954 trip, a son is briefly mentioned (without being named) with a hint of regret, noting that he was ten years old at the time. The NAU Cline Library Colorado Plateau digital archives contain photographs of Katie and a young "Ronnie."

The obituary in *The New York Times* includes the name of a second husband, Eugene Busch Jr. An article published in the *Arizona Daily Star* on June 16, 2015 features a reprint of an interview conducted in 1959 with Mrs. Gene Bush (Katie) in Holmdel, NJ. Katie and Bush were married in

---

[287] "Katie Lee (Singer)." Wikipedia.
[288] Stiles, Jim. "Live! With Katie Lee."

1958. The marriage lasted three years and then Katie moved to Aspen, Colorado from New Jersey in 1961.

On a journey to Baja, California in 1968, fate brought her face to face with Edwin Carl "Brandy" Brandelius, Jr., who would later become her "last and best husband." The dedication of her book *Sandstone Seduction* stands as a testament to their love story. Brandy had emphysema and happened to be staying at this location in Mexico when the two met. Following their marriage, Katie Lee assumed the role of a step-mother to Brandy's children—Jerilyn Lee, Ken, Susie, and John Brandelius. Brandy was a war veteran, a race car driver, and announcer. Lee noted Brandy as the prime influence on finishing and publishing her first book, *Ten Thousand Goddam Cattle*. Brandy passed away in 1973.

Lee resided in Jerome, Arizona for over four decades, from 1971 until her passing in 2017. She peacefully passed away in her sleep on November 1, 2017, at the age of ninety-eight. Lee's partner, Joey van Leeuwen, whom she met in 1979 in Australia while on a round-the-world trip, tragically passed away by suicide the day after her death. Katie and Joey were cremated and their ashes were scattered on the San Juan River.[289]

---

[289] "Katie Lee (Singer)." Wikipedia.

xlii. Harold Peary who portrayed Honest Harold and his wife Gloria Holliday who depicted Gloria the switchboard operator on the Harold Peary Show on CBS. Circa 1951. Public domain.

xliii. Harold Peary working on The Harold Peary Show for CBS in 1951. Public domain.

The Harold Peary Show

From Summerfield to Melrose Springs

Network radio underwent a dramatic transformation in the years 1948–1950 when CBS hired a number of well-known actors from NBC, a move known as the "talent raids." Among the notable individuals who made the switch were Jack Benny, Red Skelton, Edgar Bergen, and the dynamic husband-and-wife duo of George Burns and Gracie Allen. As a result, CBS had twelve out of the top fifteen radio programs by the end of 1949.[290]

There have been numerous explanations provided for Harold Peary's departure. One explanation was that he had a strong desire to showcase his singing abilities on the show, but unfortunately, Gildersleeve's production team had limitations on how much singing he could do. Additionally, CBS was attracting talent from NBC by offering more lucrative contracts. With the promise of greater financial rewards and increased artistic freedom, Peary embarked on a new venture with a different network.[291] While Harold Peary made a transition to CBS, the show he starred in, *The Great Gildersleeve*, continued to air on NBC. Harold set about creating a new series called *The Harold Peary Show*, while Willard Waterman was brought in to take over for Peary in *The Great Gildersleeve*.[292]

The *Harold Peary Show*, also known as *Honest Harold* or *The Hal Peary Show*, entertained audiences on CBS for a brief but memorable season,

---

[290] "The Harold Peary Show." Wikipedia, Wikimedia Foundation, 23 Nov. 2023.
[291] Yours Truly Johnny Blogger. "Harold Peary's Honest Mistake." The Great Detectives of Old Time Radio, 29 Jan. 1970.
[292] "The Harold Peary Show." Wikipedia.

spanning from September 17, 1950 to June 13, 1951. The scripts were crafted by Peary and a talented group of writers including Gene Stone, Bill Danch, and Jack Robinson. The plot showcased a radio show within a radio show. Harold Hemp, also known as "Honest Harold," was the charismatic host of the program *The Happy Homemaker*. During its ten a.m. airing, the show was very popular with the ladies of Melrose Springs, including the wife of the owner of the radio station where Harold works. Harold captivated the ladies with his melodic tunes and practical advice for the home. Harold's assistant on the program was Little Billy, a former horse jockey, who had a strikingly similar voice to Leroy Forrester on *The Great Gildersleeve*. Even his witty remarks evoked the essence of the character. Harold resided on 8th Avenue with his widowed elderly mother. The humor in the episodes stemmed from Hemp's interactions with other people, as one would expect from a situation comedy. The cast of characters consisted of Harold's mother, his nephew, a veterinarian, a marshal, the station manager where Harold worked, the switchboard operator, and Harold's girlfriends.[293]

Every small town in the U.S. has its own unique charm, and Melrose Springs was no exception. In the town, the presence of four cars and a bicycle were enough to be considered heavy traffic. There was only one radio station and one newspaper in town, both under the ownership of a man named Aloysius Caruthers. He insisted on being addressed by his military title, Major. Stanley Peabody, the manager at the radio station, happened to be his wife's nephew.

---

[293] "The Harold Peary Show." Wikipedia.

While not a perfect imitation, *The Harold Peary Show* was strikingly similar to *The Great Gildersleeve*. The new show even incorporated several story techniques from Gildersleeve, such as mayoral campaigns and engagements with two ladies, apparently in an attempt to replicate the success of *The Great Gildersleeve*. They went so far as to include actress Shirley Mitchell, who essentially reprised her role as Leila Ransom from *The Great Gildersleeve*, but with the character name changed to Florabelle Breckenridge.[294]

The writers and directors were fully committed to creating a vibrant supporting cast, focusing on eliciting laughter rather than exploring the deeper human qualities of their characters. There was a good deal of forced and over-the-top humor. The characters of veterinarian Doc "Yak Yak" Yancey and Mrs. Hemp's suitor, Ogleby, on *The Harold Peary Show* lacked the human quirks demonstrated by Judge Hooker and Mr. Peavey on *The Great Gildersleeve*.[295] Consequently, the program failed to garner a substantial listenership.[296] Part of the problem was that the program seemed to lack originality and excitement. As a result, both Harold Peary and CBS suffered a catastrophic outcome from the move.[297]

Although *The Harold Peary Show* had its flaws, it did possess some redeeming qualities. First came the mesmerizing performance of Peary himself. He consistently exerted maximum effort in performing the material that was provided to him. In addition, his singing voice was truly remarkable and added a delightful touch to most of the episodes.[298]

---

[294] "The Harold Peary Show." Wikipedia.
[295] Stumpf, Charles, and Ben Ohmart. "The Great Gildersleeve."
[296] "The Harold Peary Show." Wikipedia.
[297] "The Harold Peary Show." Wikipedia.
[298] Yours Truly Johnny Blogger. "Harold Peary's Honest Mistake."

There was also an emotional component to the program. The show's most heartfelt moments came in the later episodes when Harold's cousin Marvin visited. Peary read the now-famous Alan Beck piece "What is a Boy" in two different episodes and used the show to raise awareness of the Boys Club of America.[299]

> *Between the innocence of babyhood and the dignity of manhood we find a delightful creature called a boy. Boys come in assorted sizes, weights, and colors, but all boys have the same creed: to enjoy every second of every minute of every hour of every day and to protest with noise (their only weapon) when their last minute is finished and the adult males pack them off to bed at night.*
>
> *Boys are found everywhere—on top of, underneath, inside of, climbing on, swinging from, running around, or jumping to.*
>
> *Mothers love them, little girls hate them, older sisters and brothers tolerate them, adults ignore them, and Heaven protects them.*[300]

Peary graciously invited the audience to contribute gifts for Korean War veterans at the end of the program, promising to personally distribute them. Finally, he acknowledged one boy or girl in each state for their acts of honesty toward the end of the program's run.[301]

CBS had entered into a seven-year contract with Peary, stipulating that he would develop a new program and a new character exclusively for the

---

[299] Yours Truly Johnny Blogger.
[300] Beck, Alan. "What Is a Boy?" www.appleseeds.org.
[301] Yours Truly Johnny Blogger.

network. *The Harold Peary Show* was sustained by CBS for the entire season, as it was unable to secure a sponsor. Ultimately, the series failed to attain the same level of success as *The Great Gildersleeve* and subsequently faded away.[302]

---

[302] "The Harold Peary Show." Wikipedia.

Characters and Cast

Harold Hemp
Harold Peary

Mrs. Hemp (Harold's mother)
Kathryn Card
Jane Morgan

Marvin (Harold's nephew)
Sammy Ogg

Gloria (switchboard operator)
Gloria Holliday

Doctor "Yak Yak" Yancey (veterinarian)
Joseph Kearns

Pete the Marshal
Parley Baer

Stanley Peabody (station manager)
Olan Soule

Miss Turner (the teacher)
June Whitley

Evelina (Harold's girlfriend and Doctor Yancey's niece)
Mary Jane Croft

xliv. Kathryn Card and Charles Cooper in How to Marry a Millionaire (1957). Public domain

Kathryn Card

Kathryn Card who originally played Mrs. Hemp, Harold Hemp's mother, on *The Harold Peary Show* was an American radio, television, and film actress who may be best remembered for her role as Mrs. McGillicuddy, Lucy's mother on *I Love Lucy*.

Kathryn was born Kathryn Rose Sheehan in Butte, Montana, on October 4, 1892. She was one of four children born to Irish immigrant parents Richard Sheehan and Esther McCurdy. Card had a variety of radio roles in the late 1930s, including *Uncle Walter's Doghouse*, *The Bartons*, *Just Neighbors*, *Girl Alone*, *The Woman in White*, and *Story of Mary Marlin*. In 1943, she joined the cast of *Helpmate*, a daytime serial on NBC.

Her first film credit was in 1945 for her role as Louise in the Corliss Archer movie *Kiss and Tell*, starring Shirley Temple as Corliss Archer. The next year, she appeared in *Undercurrent* with Robert Taylor, Katharine Hepburn, and Robert Mitchum. Card also had a small role as a landlady of the Oleander Arms Hotel in the 1954 Warner Bros. remake of *A Star Is Born*. Her part consisted of one scene early in the film. Soon after the movie was released, Warner Bros. made significant edits to the film, resulting in Card's part being completely omitted. In 1983, Ronald Haver, a film historian, made an incredible discovery. He managed to find the original monaural three-hour soundtrack and a majority of the missing footage. He proceeded to create replicas of the scene, using a different actress to replace Card, while synchronizing the dialogue on the soundtrack.

On February 8, 1954, Card made her first television appearance in an episode of *I Love Lucy*. In the installment titled "Fan Magazine Interview," Card portrayed the character of Minnie Finch, a woman with a rather disheveled appearance. In the following year, she found herself playing a completely different role—that of Mrs. McGillicuddy, Lucy's scatterbrained mother.

She portrayed the character in five episodes during the 1954-1955 season and made three more appearances during the 1955-1956 season when the Ricardos and the Mertzes traveled to Europe. Surprisingly, Card's character mysteriously vanished from the story after both couples relocated to Connecticut the following year. She took on that role one final time in an episode of *The Lucille Ball-Desi Arnaz Show* called "The Ricardos Go to Japan" in 1959.

Apart from *I Love Lucy*, Card guest-starred on other television shows including *Perry Mason*, *The George Burns and Gracie Allen Show*, *Make Room for Daddy*, *Alfred Hitchcock Presents*, and *Rawhide*.[303]

Kathryn Card made her final film appearance as Mrs. Wadlington in the 1964 MGM musical *The Unsinkable Molly Brown*.

Kathryn Sheehan married Erwin Foster Card on October 4, 1910, and they had a daughter, Ada Ester Card, who was born in 1912 and died in 1943. Kathryn and Erwin divorced in 1914. On March 1, 1964, Card died as a result of a fatal heart attack at the age of seventy-one at her home in Costa Mesa, California.[304]

---

[303] "Kathryn Card." Wikipedia, Wikimedia Foundation, 18 Mar. 2024.
[304] IMDb. "Kathryn Card - Biography." IMDb, IMDb.com.

xlv. From left to rightt: Jane Morgan, Robert Rockwell, Gloria McMillan, Richard Crenna, Eve Arden and Gale Gordon from Our Miss Brooks. Public domain.

xlvi. Jane Morgan. Public domain.

Jane Morgan

British-born Jane Morgan, the second actress to play the role of Harold Hemp's mother on *The Harold Peary Show*, had a very unique and recognizable voice that was frequently heard on the radio. However, she first gained recognition as a violinist and classical singer, performing on stage and in concert halls. She made her radio debut in 1930.[305]

Morgan was born in Warmley, Gloucestershire, to Welsh parents on December 6, 1880. She crossed the Atlantic to Boston with her family at the age of one.[306] Jane's childhood ambition was to become a concert violinist, and she pursued her goal by enrolling in the New England Conservatory of Music. She incorporated voice training into her curriculum and, upon her graduation, became a violinist-singer at the Boston Opera Company, earning $25 per week. Jane focused on honing her acting abilities to meet the demands of operatic roles, which often call for a certain level of dramatic interpretation.[307]

From 1900 to 1901, she lived in Anaconda, Montana, with her father Roderick "Rod" Morgan and older brother Charles following the death of her mother. There, she met the man she would eventually marry, twenty-three-year-old Albion, Wisconsin native, Leo Cullen Bryant. He taught music and led the Margaret Theater Orchestra.[308]

---

[305] Shreve, Ivan G. "Happy Birthday, Jane Morgan!" Radio Spirits, 16 Dec. 2019.
[306] "Jane Morgan (Actress)." Wikipedia, Wikimedia Foundation, 20 July 2024.
[307] Shreve, Ivan G. "Happy Birthday, Jane Morgan!"
[308] "Jane Morgan (Actress)." Wikipedia.

Soon after their marriage on February 17, 1901, the Bryants established a music school in Butte, Montana, specializing in piano and violin instruction.[309] A few years later, they moved their business to Nampa, Idaho, and Jane embarked on a career in vaudeville, performing in a variety of musical comedies and dramas such as *The Master Mind* (1914), *The Silent Voice* (1914), and *Her Temporary Husband* (1926). She co-starred with Charlotte Greenwood in *She Couldn't Say No* (1930) and with Barbara Stanwyck in *Tattle Tales* (1933). She later pursued a career in radio acting, joining *Lux Radio Theatre's* stock company and making guest appearances on shows such as *Dr. Christian*.[310]

She gained recognition in the world of radio through her role in *Point Sublime*, a comedy-drama set in a quaint seaport village. The show revolved around the romantic relationship between Evelyn "Evy" Hanover (played by Jane) and Ben Willet, the storekeeper and mayor (played by Cliff Arquette). Earle Ross, Verna Felton, Lou Merrill, and Mel Blanc were notable members of the cast of Sublime, which aired on NBC's West Coast network from 1940 to 1942. Morgan's voice was also heard daily in the role of Aunt Mary on the program with the same name, where the main character bore some resemblance to Ma Perkins. The show aired from 1942 to 1952.[311]

On *The Jack Benny Program*, Jane Morgan and Gloria Gordon, who is Gale's mother, portrayed Martha and Emily, two devoted elderly fans. Jane initially portrayed the character of landlady Kathleen O'Reilly on the popular radio show *My Friend Irma*. However, she later decided to

---

[309] "Jane Morgan (Actress)." Wikipedia.
[310] Shreve, Ivan G. "Happy Birthday, Jane Morgan!"
[311] Shreve, Ivan G. "Happy Birthday, Jane Morgan!"

pass on the role to Gloria. Gordon and Morgan shared similar backgrounds, both being born in England and launching their show business careers through their music studies.[312]

Jane's other regular appearances include the role of the eccentric Mrs. Foster on Jack Carson's program *The Sealtest Village Store*, a diverse array of roles on Bob Hope's program, and the succession of Kathryn Card as Mother Hemp on *The Harold Peary Show* on November 1, 1950.[313]

However, the radio role for which Jane Morgan is most fondly remembered is that of Margaret Davis, the pixilated landlady of schoolteacher Connie Brooks in the popular radio sitcom *Our Miss Brooks*. Jane became so closely identified with Mrs. Davis that she easily made the transition with the radio cast to television. She subsequently reprised her role in the 1956 film adaptation. It was her only film credit.[314]

Jane Morgan was a versatile radio performer who also had various non-comedic roles on a variety of shows, including *The Adventures of Philip Marlowe, Arch Oboler's Plays, Boston Blackie, Broadway's My Beat, The Cavalcade of America, Encore Theatre, The Eternal Light, The First Nighter Program, The Ford Theatre, Hallmark Playhouse, Hedda Hopper's Hollywood, Hollywood Star Playhouse, Hollywood Star Time, The Lady Esther/Camel Screen Guild Theatre, Let George Do It, Lights Out, The Man Called X, Mystery in the Air, Night Beat, Presenting Charles Boyer, Richard Diamond, Private Detective, Screen Director's*

---

[312] Shreve, Ivan G. "Happy Birthday, Jane Morgan!"
[313] "Jane Morgan: Radio Star: Old Time Radio Downloads." Jane Morgan | Radio Star | Old Time Radio Downloads.
[314] Shreve, Ivan G. "Happy Birthday, Jane Morgan!"

Playhouse, *The Skippy Hollywood Theatre, Suspense,* and *The Whistler.*[315]

She made the decision to retire from the entertainment industry following the final airing of the last radio episode of *Our Miss Brooks* in 1957. She was confined to her bed for the last five years of her life due to a prolonged struggle with heart disease. She passed away in 1972 at the age of ninety-one.[316]

---

[315] "Jane Morgan: Radio Star: Old Time Radio Downloads."
[316] Shreve, Ivan G. "Happy Birthday, Jane Morgan!"

xlvii. CBS publicity photo featuring Gloria Holliday at the information desk. Circa 1944. Public domain.

xlviii. Gloria Holliday. Circa 1950. Public domain.

Gloria Holliday

It is indeed true that there is a noticeable resemblance between the switchboard operator, Gloria, on *The Harold Peary Show* and Throckmorton P. Gildersleeve's incompetent secretary Bessie on *The Great Gildersleeve*. Gloria Holliday, who happened to be Harold Peary's second wife in real life, took on the challenge of portraying both characters.

In the autumn of 1942, Throckmorton P. Gildersleeve assumed the role of Summerfield's water commissioner and was entrusted with the responsibility of overseeing the town's water supply. As part of his new position, he also gained the services of Ms. Fitch, who had previously served as the secretary to the former water commissioner. Ms. Fitch had a long tenure as a city employee and had the unique distinction of being the daughter of Summerfield's first water commissioner. Gildersleeve masterfully orchestrated the replacement of the woman with a much younger and more attractive individual named Bessie Barstow. Pauline Drake was the first actress who brought the character of Bessie to life. In December 1945, Gloria Holliday assumed the role.[317]

Holliday was a talented singer and actress who was born in Billings, Montana on August 26, 1924. In 1932, her family made the bold decision to move to California. Gloria had always dreamed of a career in acting, fueled by her deep passion for the world of cinema. Right after graduating from North Hollywood High School in 1943, she landed a job in the CBS

---

[317] Stumpf, Charles, and Ben Ohmart. The Great Gildersleeve, BearManor Media, Boalsburg, PA, 2002, p. 34.

mail room. She quickly caught the attention of producer Fran Van Hartesveldt, who was involved in the creation of *The Kate Smith Hour*. From 1937 to 1945, *The Kate Smith Hour* was the undisputed champion of radio variety shows, offering a captivating mix of comedy, music, and drama. Kate Smith (May 1, 1907 – June 17, 1986) was a highly acclaimed singer, often referred to as the "First Lady of Radio." She garnered widespread admiration during the war years. Van Hartesveldt recruited Gloria to take on various roles on the program.[318]

Upon learning of the opening for the character of Bessie in *The Great Gildersleeve* series, Van Hartesveldt enthusiastically encouraged Gloria to try out for the part. Harold Peary was conspicuously absent and had no say in her immediate hiring. Gloria's first performance was an absolute catastrophe, as she was struck by an unfortunate bout of appendicitis, causing her to fumble over a line. Peary was filled with frustration and insisted that the producers let her go. But after learning about her illness, he had a change of heart.[319]

Gloria decided to follow Peary when he moved from NBC to CBS. Despite the short-lived run of *The Harold Peary Show* on CBS, their artistic collaboration continued. Together, they formed a musical act that made its grand debut at the renowned Coronado Hotel in San Diego. Peary sang as Gloria skillfully played the piano. For nearly a year, they traveled to different venues, including the Shamrock Hotel in San Antonio, Texas.

---

[318] Stumpf, Charles, and Ben Ohmart. The Great Gildersleeve, pp. 119-120.
[319] Stumpf, Charles, and Ben Ohmart. The Great Gildersleeve, pp. 119-120.

After her divorce from Peary in 1956, she wholeheartedly devoted herself to music. In addition to her performances at various local clubs, she also showcased her piano skills at several hotels near Los Angeles International Airport. Over the course of the next five years, she embarked on a journey to establish herself as a professional musician.[320]

Once Gloria's time in the spotlight had faded, she reunited with her former high school sweetheart, Ray McGalliard. The pair spent their days exploring diverse destinations across the globe.[321]

---

[320] Stumpf, Charles, and Ben Ohmart. The Great Gildersleeve, pp. 119-120.
[321] Stumpf, Charles, and Ben Ohmart. The Great Gildersleeve, pp. 119-120.

xlix. Joseph Kearns. Public domain.

Joseph Kearns

Joseph Kearns is generally recognized as the grouchy, cantankerous neighbor George Wilson on CBS's *Dennis the Menace*. Kearns, who began his acting journey in 1916 with "The Rising Generation," a vaudeville troupe of eleven children, enjoyed a successful television career in the 1950s and early 60s. He appeared in a range of popular programs such as *The Jack Benny Program*, *Our Miss Brooks*, *The George Burns and Gracie Allen Show*, *The Adventures of Ozzie and Harriet*, *I Love Lucy*, *My Little Margie*, *Perry Mason*, *I Married Joan*, and *Gunsmoke*.[322]

He achieved great success as a radio actor in the 1940s, playing in numerous popular shows such as *The Adventures of Sam Spade*, *Burns and Allen*, *The Whistler*, *Suspense*, *The New Adventures of Sherlock Holmes*, and portraying the veterinarian Doctor "Yak Yak" Yancey on *The Harold Peary Show*.[323] Doc Yancey's character bore a striking resemblance to Judge Hooker from *The Great Gildersleeve*. He was an elderly gentleman who had a knack for speaking his mind to Harold. He even let out a cackle reminiscent of the old judge in Summerfield. Harold referred to him as a "horse doctor" just like Gildersleeve had called the judge an "old goat." Due to his more than casual interest in his niece Evelina, Harold paid frequent visits to the Yancey residence.

---

[322] "Joseph Kearns." Wikipedia, Wikimedia Foundation, 2 Mar. 2024.
[323] "Joseph Kearns." Wikipedia.

Joseph Sherrard Kearns grew up in a family deeply rooted in their Mormon faith, with his parents Joseph Albert Kearns, a wool buyer, and Cordelia Marie Peterson, a talented concert pianist.[324] His mother schooled him as a pianist and organist when he was a child, and he developed a love for music that lasted the rest of his lifetime. After graduating from the University of Utah with a music degree, he went to work for his father's Boston-based wool company, despite the fact that the prospect of spending his life doing what his father did for a profession did not appeal to him. He also worked as a movie theater organist.[325]

Then Kearns made a mistake that ruined his wool business career. He purchased $8,000 worth of exotic fleece and shipped it back to the headquarters, only to be told that the company had no use for undyeable black wool. Joseph Kearns left the wool business, a decision his father wholeheartedly supported, and joined a California theatrical group in 1935.[326]

He eagerly embraced every role that came his way, just like any other versatile performer in a stock company. He set off on tours with roadshow versions of the most popular plays of the time, perfecting his knack for using his distinct voice to its maximum potential. He may not have fit the mold of a classic heartthrob, but he soon discovered that the real magic of a production comes from the talented character actors who infuse it with depth and energy.[327]

---

[324] "Joseph Kearns." Wikipedia.
[325] "Joseph 'Mr. Wilson' Kearns Doesn't Mind Playing Straight Man to a Child Actor-He Was Once One Himself." TV Guide, 15 July 1961.
[326] "Joseph 'Mr. Wilson' Kearns Doesn't Mind Playing Straight Man to a Child Actor-He Was Once One Himself."
[327] "Joseph 'Mr. Wilson' Kearns Doesn't Mind Playing Straight Man to a Child Actor-He Was Once One Himself."

The surge in radio's popularity was driven by actors like Joseph Kearns, who possessed both youthful enthusiasm and came with a budget-friendly price tag. As network radio shifted its base from New York and Chicago to the film capital, Kearns quickly established himself as a sought-after talent in the Hollywood radio directory. He found himself in a perpetual rivalry with Hanley Stafford and Gale Gordon, as they all portrayed a multitude of uptight and easily provoked authority figures that were frequently encountered by the comedians of that time.

He was a regular presence on popular radio shows like *Burns and Allen*, *Judy Canova*, *Jack Benny*, *Scattergood Baines*, and *Fibber McGee and Molly*. On the *Suspense* series, he was the eerie individual who introduced listeners to "A tale well calculated to keep you in SUSPENSE." He also played the role of Ed the vault keeper on Jack Benny's TV show and portrayed the hotel manager on *How to Marry a Millionaire*.[328]

Kearns flourished in the fifties as a highly regarded member of the CBS-Hollywood stock company, allowing him to fulfill a long-held dream. CBS managed to get their hands on a magnificent Wurlitzer theatre organ from Warner Bros. Pictures, all set to be installed in the prestigious Columbia Square studios. Nevertheless, thanks to the increasing popularity of the compact and budget-friendly Hammond electric organ as a go-to option for fill music, the network made the decision to stow away the instrument. The colossal Wurlitzer was ultimately bound for the scrapyard. Kearns had a soft spot for theatre organs, so when he found

---

[328] "Joseph 'Mr. Wilson' Kearns Doesn't Mind Playing Straight Man to a Child Actor-He Was Once One Himself."

out the network was planning to get rid of one, he wasted no time in making a very tempting cash offer.[329]

After recognizing that he lacked a suitable location to store the instrument and was single with no one else to consider, he resolved to construct an entire house in 1955 to accommodate the organ. An extraordinary two-and-a-half-story cube, the structure, which remains in place at 6126 Carlos Avenue in Hollywood, California, was constructed with soundproofing and pipes in the walls. In order to accommodate the substantial weight of the organ console and chests, special steel pillars and girders were used. The console was the primary focal point of the living room.[330] Regrettably, the pipe organ and all of its hardware, which were concealed between the walls, were removed by the subsequent owners after Joseph Kearns' death in 1962. The Renaissance Theatre in Mansfield, Ohio, became the new home of Kearns' cherished pipe organ.

Joseph Kearns had a successful television career during a time when radio was losing its charm. His performances in situation comedies left a lasting impression, and his role on *Dennis the Menace* in 1959 was a standout moment in his career. At first, Mr. Wilson was just another minor role for Kearns. He was given a five-year contract and guaranteed a part in seven out of every thirteen episodes. After leaving Mr. Wilson out of three episodes in the first season, Screen Gems came to the realization that there were no other cast members for Dennis to menace. Consequently, Mr. Wilson has been featured in every episode filmed since. According to producer Jim Fonda, "Mr. Wilson was to Dennis what Amos was to

---

[329] "Joseph 'Mr. Wilson' Kearns Doesn't Mind Playing Straight Man to a Child Actor-He Was Once One Himself."
[330] "Joseph 'Mr. Wilson' Kearns Doesn't Mind Playing Straight Man to a Child Actor-He Was Once One Himself."

Andy." During an interview in 1961 regarding his role in the program, Kearns stated, "If I'd known it, I could have got more money. Every time I think about that contract, I feel as if I'd bought five more carloads of black wool."[331]

Kearns experienced a cerebral hemorrhage on February 11, 1962, while filming the third season of *Dennis the Menace*. He was hospitalized in a coma and unfortunately never regained consciousness. Kearns passed away on February 17, 1962, just five days after his fifty-fifth birthday. His death was believed by some to be caused by the Metrecal diet he was following. Reports indicate that he was able to lose an impressive forty pounds in a mere six weeks.[332]

Following Kearns' passing, Gale Gordon stepped in as John, George Wilson's brother, in the *Dennis the Menace* cast.[333]

---

[331] "Joseph 'Mr. Wilson' Kearns Doesn't Mind Playing Straight Man to a Child Actor-He Was Once One Himself."
[332] "Joseph Kearns." Wikipedia.
[333] "Joseph Kearns." Wikipedia.

1. Joseph Kearns' beloved pipe organ photographed in 1957.

li.Situated on the opposite wall from the console, a grill conceals the organ chambers in Kearns' living room. Circa 1957.

lii. The Kearns residence circa 1957.

liii. Willard Waterman and Parley Baer during a rehearsal for The First Nighter. Circa 1948. Public domain.

liv. Parley Bear circa 1940s. Public domain.

Parley Baer

Parley Baer may not have been a household name, but his face and voice left a lasting impression on viewers and listeners for generations. Throughout his illustrious career spanning six decades, he had the honor of bringing to life the character Pete the Marshall on the short-lived CBS sitcom *The Harold Peary Show*. His talent and versatility shone through as he graced the screens in over sixty movies and an impressive sixteen hundred television programs.[334]

Parley, like Joseph Kearns, was a native of Salt Lake City. In 1933, he began working at the local radio station KSL after completing his studies in drama at the University of Utah. Additionally, he served as a circus ringmaster and publicist.[335] Baer joined the Army Air Corps during World War II and, as a captain, received seven combat honors for his exceptional service in the Pacific Theater. In 1946, following the war, Parley married Ernestine Clarke, who had previously worked as a circus aerialist and bareback rider.[336]

He established himself as a radio fixture after relocating to Los Angeles in 1947. He appeared on a variety of programs, including *The Count of Monte Cristo*, *Lux Radio Theater*, *Screen Directors' Playhouse*, *Cisco Kid*, *Red Ryder*, *My Friend Irma*, and *My Favorite Husband*.[337] He subsequently depicted a multitude of characters in fifteen thousand radio

---

[334] Utah-Born Actor Dies in California at 88." Deseret News, Deseret News, 3 Dec. 2002.
[335] "Parley Baer." Variety, 26 Nov. 2002.
[336] Harrigan, Tom. "Character Actor Baer Dies at 88." The Napa Valley Register, 24 Nov. 2002.
[337] Utah-Born Actor Dies in California at 88."

broadcasts. Undoubtedly, the most memorable part was that of Chester Proudfoot in the original rendition of *Gunsmoke*.[338]

With the advent of television in the early 1950s, he gained recognition for portraying authoritative figures. He made appearances and had recurring roles on numerous series such as *Dragnet, Lassie, Father Knows Best, I Love Lucy, You Are There,* and *Perry Mason*. He gained fame for his memorable roles in *The Andy Griffith Show* as Mayor Stoner and in *The Adventures of Ozzie and Harriet* as Darby, Ozzie Nelson's neighbor.[339] Additionally, he provided the voice of one of the Keebler Cookie elves.[340]

Aside from his acting jobs, Parley engaged in training and working with lions and tigers at the former Jungleland in Thousand Oaks. He also served on the board of L.A. Circus and volunteered as a docent at the Los Angeles Zoo.[341]

Baer worked steadily in motion pictures and television until the end of his career. He appeared in *Dave* (1993) alongside Kevin Kline, *Last of the Dogmen* (1995) playing against Tom Berenger, and the TV series *Beverly Hills 90210* and *Star Trek: Voyager*. He also began a lengthy tenure on the daytime soap opera *The Young and the Restless* in 1993, where he portrayed the senior citizen, Miles Dugan. In 1997, Baer's career ended abruptly due to a stroke that impaired his speech.[342]

Regrettably, Parley passed away on November 22, 2002, at the Motion Picture and Television Hospital in Woodland Hills due to complications

---

[338] Utah-Born Actor Dies in California at 88."
[339] "Parley Baer- Biography." Turner Classic Movies.
[340] "Utah-Born Actor Dies in California at 88."
[341] "Parley Baer." Variety.
[342] "Parley Baer- Biography.".

resulting from a second stroke he sustained on November 11. He was never able to completely recover from the first stroke in 1997. He was eighty-eight years old.[343]

---

[343] "Parley Baer." Variety.

lv. Willard Waterman, Barbara Luddy and Olan Soule on The First Nighter. Courtesy of Mary Anna Waterman.

Olan Soule

Illinois native Olan Soule had an extensive career in the entertainment industry. He appeared in nearly seven thousand radio shows and commercials, two hundred television series and television films, and in over sixty movies. One of his notable roles was as Mr. Stanley Peabody, the radio station manager on *The Harold Peary Show*.[344] Stanley Peabody was a man who exuded an air of superiority, thanks in part to the support of his aunt's husband, Aloysius Caruthers, the proprietor of the town's only radio station. Mr. Caruthers, a seasoned military veteran with a strong sense of discipline, held a rather low opinion of his nephew, which occasionally proved to be advantageous for Harold. Stanley and Harold were constantly at odds, much like the rivalry between Gildersleeve and his wealthy neighbor Rumson Bullard.

Olan Evart Soule discovered his love for writing and dramatics in high school. At just seventeen years old, he began touring the Midwest with the renowned Jack Brooks stock company playing juvenile leads, singing, dancing, playing drums, driving trucks, and erecting the tents six nights a week for $35.[345] He continued to work with similar repertory troupes, but by 1931, many of these touring productions had closed their doors. The Great Depression had swallowed the country. Olan and his wife Norma Elizabeth Miller moved to New York, where Olan secured employment operating elevators and serving hamburgers alongside fellow unemployed actors in the city. After two years, Soule landed in Chicago,

---

[344] "Olan Soule." Wikipedia, Wikimedia Foundation, 10 May 2024.
[345] Oliver, Myrna. "Olan Soule; Actor's Versatile Voice Led to Multimedia Career." Los Angeles Times, Los Angeles Times, 4 Feb. 1994.

working as a secretary-switchboard operator-file clerk. Following his dismissal from the job, he made the decision to pursue his deep-seated passion for the performing arts.[346]

Olan Soule kicked off his radio career in 1933 on station KSO in Des Moines, Iowa. However, his first venture into the world of dramatic acting occurred on Chicago's WGN, where he made an appearance on *Uncle Quin's Scalawags*. Following that, Olan secured a recurring role on *Painted Dreams*. Soule quickly established himself as a highly sought-after and dependable actor in Chicago. He portrayed Bob Regent on *Chandu the Magician*, Coach Hardy on *Jack Armstrong, the All-American Boy*, and Chinese cook Aha on *Little Orphan Annie*. He also made appearances on various popular radio shows and theater productions, including *Author's Playhouse*, *The Chicago Theatre of the Air*, *The Couple Next Door*, *Curtain Time*, *Fifth Row Center*, *Freedom of Opportunity*, *Grand Hotel*, *Grand Marquee*, *Jenny Peabody*, *Midstream*, *The Story of Joan and Kermit*, *A Tale of Today*, *Tom Mix and His Ralston Straight Shooters*, *Valiant Lady*, and *The Wayside Theatre*.[347]

In 1943, Olan Soule became a member of the cast of *The First Nighter Program*. Three years later, he took on the role of the show's leading man, starring alongside Barbara Luddy.[348] In 1947, he moved with the show to Hollywood.[349] As radio drama waned, he showcased his talent in various films and television shows, earning a reputation as a dependable character actor. Soule mentioned that due to his physical appearance and glasses,

---

[346] Shreve, Ivan G. "Happy Birthday, Olan Soule!" Radio Spirits, 28 Feb. 2021.
[347] Shreve, Ivan G. "Happy Birthday, Olan Soule!"
[348] Shreve, Ivan G. "Happy Birthday, Olan Soule!"
[349] Oliver, Myrna. "Olan Soule."

he was primarily cast as lab technicians, newscasters, and railroad clerks.[350]

Soule played Tut on *Captain Midnight*, choir director John Masters on *The Andy Griffith Show*, and had roles on *I Love Lucy, The Jack Benny Show, The Burns and Allen Show, The Twilight Zone, Dallas, The Love Boat, Fantasy Island*, and *Simon and Simon* in addition to his role in the long-running *Dragnet*, in which he performed with his friend Jack Webb on radio, television, and two feature films. He continued to provide the voice for Batman in the animated series *Super Friends* until 1984, at which point he was seventy-five years old. Among Soule's films were *North by Northwest, Days of Wine and Roses, The Towering Inferno*, and *The Apple Dumpling Gang*.[351]

From 1954 to 1956, he was the president of the American Federation of Television and Radio Artists Hollywood local and established its pension and welfare fund.[352]

Sadly, Soule lost his battle with lung cancer and passed away on February 1, 1994, at the home of his daughter in Corona, California. He was eighty-four years old.[353]

---

[350] Olan Soule." Wikipedia.
[351] Oliver, Myrna. "Olan Soule."
[352] Oliver, Myrna.
[353] Oliver, Myrna.

lvi. Mary Jane Croft. Public domain.

Mary Jane Croft

Mary Jane Croft, known for her role as Evelina, Harold Hemp's romantic partner, on *The Harold Peary Show*, started her acting career in the local civic theatre in her hometown.[354] She described herself as "a stage-struck 17-year-old just out of high school." "From 1935 to 1939, I played parts with every kind of voice and accent: children, babies, old women, society belles, main street floozies – everything," she reminisced.[355] She was born in Muncie, Indiana, on February 15, 1916, and later became highly involved in network radio during the 30s and 40s. Prior to that, she had a brief stint in acting with the Guild Theatre in Cincinnati, Ohio. Afterwards, she joined local radio station WLW and began her journey as a radio actress.

After her marriage to fellow actor, Jack Zoller, she relocated to Los Angeles in 1939.[356] Throughout the 1940s and 50s, Mary Jane made frequent appearances on popular radio shows such as *Life with Luigi, Blondie, The Adventures of Sam Spade, Suspense, The Beulah Show, The Bill Goodwin Show, Broadway Is My Beat, On Stage, Crime Classics, Four-Star Playhouse, The Harold Peary Show, Joan Davis Time, The Mel Blanc Show, One Man's Family, Our Miss Brooks*, and *Sears Radio Theater*. She also made guest appearances on Lucille Ball's *My Favorite Husband*, which marked the start of their subsequent professional and personal relationship.[357]

---

[354] "Mary Jane Croft." 2018 Writing Her Story, Indiana Commission for Women.
[355] "Mary Jane Croft." Papermoon Loves Lucy, Tumbler, 12 Feb. 2018.
[356] "Mary Jane Croft." 2018 Writing Her Story.
[357] "Mary Jane Croft." Wikipedia, Wikimedia Foundation, 6 Apr. 2024.

From 1962 to 1974, she played sidekick roles alongside Lucille Ball in the popular television series *I Love Lucy* and *Here's Lucy*.[358] She also appeared on sitcoms like *Our Miss Brooks* and *The Adventures of Ozzie and Harriett*.[359] Croft made an unsold pilot called *The Two of Us*, which focused on the life of a children's book illustrator. The pilot was created by Desilu, the production company established by Lucille Ball and her husband Desi Arnaz.[360]

She pursued her acting career on television for several years following the conclusion of *Here's Lucy*, even sharing the screen with Ball once again in 1977 for the special "Lucy Calls the President." In 1979, she made a comeback to radio by appearing in several episodes of *Sears Radio Theater*.[361]

After her divorce from Jack Zoller, Mary Jane married Elliott Lewis, an American actor, and former husband of Cathy Lewis. They remained happily married until his passing in 1990. Croft's first marriage produced a son, Eric, who was killed in action during the Vietnam War in 1967.[362]

After her death on August 24, 1999, Lucie Arnaz eulogized her mother's friend, Mary Jane, as being the "antithesis of the dizzy blonde she portrayed on screen" and as a fun-loving and joyous spirit.[363]

---

[358] "Mary Jane Croft." Indiana Broadcast Pioneers.
[359] "Mary Jane Croft." Papermoon Loves Lucy.
[360] "Mary Jane Croft." Wikipedia.
[361] "Mary Jane Croft." Wikipedia.
[362] "Mary Jane Croft." Wikipedia.
[363] "Mary Jane Croft." 2018 Writing Her Story.

lvii. Mary Jane Croft with Hattie McDaniel and Henry Blair on The Beulah Show, Circa 1948. Public domain.

lviii. Sammy Ogg, child actor. Circa early 1950s. Public domain.

Sammy Ogg

In contrast to Gildersleeve's nephew Leroy, who was portrayed by adult actor Walter Tetley, Harold Hemp's nephew Marvin was portrayed by child actor Sammy Ogg, who was the younger brother of actor Jimmy Ogg (1929-86). Born on October 30, 1939 in Lexington, Virginia, Ogg is best known for his roles in *Matinee Theatre* (Previously known as *Dangerously Yours*), *I Love Lucy,* and the film *The Miracle of Our Lady of Fatima* (1952).[364]

Ogg made his screen debut in 1947 as a street-wise tough kid (uncredited) in the film *Lost Honeymoon*, which starred Franchot Tone. At the time, he was only seven years old. In 1951, he made two additional uncredited film appearances: *Week-end with Father* and *The Day the Earth Stood Still*. Additionally, he played an uncredited role in Cecil B. DeMille's *The Greatest Show on Earth*. Lucille Ball was cast in the 1952 film; however, she was compelled to withdraw due to her pregnancy. Despite this, it was not long before Ball and Ogg would share the screen together. Ogg would go on to portray one of the mischievous Hudson twins on a memorable season one episode of *I Love Lucy*.[365]

Ogg made an appearance on *Our Miss Brooks* on Christmas Day 1953 along with Gale Gordon and an ensemble of actors from the beloved show *I Love Lucy*. The show was filmed at Desilu. The following year, he had the opportunity to perform on *The Danny Thomas Show* (also known as

---

[364] "Sammy Ogg – @papermoonloveslucy on Tumblr." Papermoon Loves Lucy, Tumbler, 30 Oct. 2020.
[365] "Sammy Ogg – @papermoonloveslucy on Tumblr."

Make Room for Danny), which was also filmed at Desilu. Sammy portrayed the first date of Terry Williams, the youngest daughter on the program. This was several years before the show changed networks and did a crossover with *The Lucy-Desi Comedy Hour*.

Between 1955 and 1957, Ogg portrayed the jokester sidekick Joe Simpson on *Spin and Marty*, a series of television shorts that aired as part of *The Mickey Mouse Club*. Even though he appeared alongside his on-screen twin, David Stollery (*I Love Lucy*), David had a prominent role as the wealthy, orphaned Martin "Marty" Markham, while Sammy was given a supporting role as Joe. Ogg appeared on the television series *Dragnet* seven times between 1952 and 1959, each time portraying a different character. His penultimate appearance came in the series *Union Pacific* alongside his older brother Jimmy Ogg. In July 1959, Ogg had his last on-screen role in *The Joseph Cotten Show: On Trial*, featuring Rod Steiger. There is limited information about Sammy Ogg's life after that, as he made the decision to leave the entertainment industry and pursue a career as a clergyman.[366]

---

[366] "Sammy Ogg – @papermoonloveslucy on Tumblr."

Legacy

Today, *The Great Gildersleeve* is recognized as one of radio's most cherished comedic figures — a genuine, kind-hearted individual who often found himself the unintentional target of his own pomposity. The program's success stemmed largely from the remarkable creativity of its writers, who crafted a setting that was incredibly vivid and characterizations that were so distinctive that they managed to overcome the loss of the show's lead actor. The production's smooth transition to a new lead, while preserving its endearing spirit and connection with the audience, is a testament to the timelessness of its themes and its exceptional writing. Gildersleeve's comedic triumphs and tribulations resonated with audiences of all ages, who recognized aspects of themselves within the character.

After an impressive seventeen-year run, *The Great Gildersleeve* leaves behind a legacy that resonates through the ages. This beloved radio show not only enchanted listeners during the 1940s and 50s, but also sparked a cultural phenomenon, inspiring radio clubs and collectors who continue to keep its spirit alive through recordings and reenactments. Additionally, with the advancements in computer technology, countless others are now discovering the pleasures of *The Great Gildersleeve* and old-time radio as a whole via mp3 files accessible on various websites devoted to this medium.

The show's influence permeates popular culture, with playful nods in various cartoons like the 1945 Bugs Bunny episode titled "Hare Conditioned." In this episode, Bugs finds himself being chased by the manager of Macy's Department Store. The manager closely resembles Harold Peary's character Throckmorton P. Gildersleeve. Bugs interrupts him, remarking that he sounds "Just like that guy on the radio: The Great

Gildersneeze!" The manager, curious, replies with an astonished "I do?!" accompanied by a laugh that echoes Gildersleeve's own chuckle. The voice actor in this instance remains uncredited, yet it is thought to be Dave Barry, who, alongside his film and television roles, contributed to cartoon voice work for Columbia, Warner Bros., Disney, Republic Pictures, and Screen Gems throughout the 1940s.

In the 1941 Warner Bros. classic titled "A Coy Decoy," Daffy Duck skillfully utilized Gildersleeve's famous phrase "You're a haa-aa-aard man!" to divert a wolf that was pursuing him. In Tex Avery's 1943 cartoon short, *One Ham's Family*, actor Kent Rogers expertly brought Gildersleeve's voice to life. Elroy Jetson, the son from Hanna-Barbera's iconic 1962 animated series *The Jetsons*, takes his name from Leroy Forrester. Elroy is an anagram of Leroy.

In August 1977, a music venue whose name was derived from the radio program, *The Great Gildersleeve*, was established in Manhattan. In February 1984, the New York City Board of Estimate acquired the building housing the club through eminent domain, leading to the venue's closure as it was repurposed as a shelter for the homeless. After a rent dispute between the building owner and the city, the latter leased three of the upper floors of the building, which was operated as the Kenton Hotel, to accommodate approximately 200 homeless males. Following the building's condemnation by the city, it was transformed into a flophouse. Project Renewal then took over establishing the Kenton Hall Men's Shelter, which served as a shelter for homeless men receiving methadone maintenance treatment.

lix. The Great Gildersleeves in New York. Cicra 1977. CC BY-NC-SA 4.0.

lx. Ad in the Village Voice for The Great Gildersleeves. October 31, 1977.

After the club's closure, Gilded Records released a compilation album called "The Best of Great Gildersleeves," featuring the bands that frequently performed at the venue. The album showcased a selection of tracks from artists such as The Privates, Didus and the Fabulous Mascarenes, along with the John Morales Band. In 2000, the band Danger Danger titled its album "The Return of the Great Gildersleeves" as an homage to the venue.

In 1944, the now defunct Street & Smith Publications featured a comic book story of *The Great Gildersleeve* in one of its issues of *Supersnipe Comics*. They included a two-page biography of actor Harold Peary, followed by a multi-page Gildersleeve story featuring Fibber McGee and Molly as guests, right in the middle of the comic book. Charles Boland, an illustrator who worked on several Street & Smith comics, such as *Doc Savage*, *Shadow Comics*, *Super Magician Comics*, and *Supersnipe Comics*, signed one of the Gildersleeve panels indicating he was the artist responsible for producing the artwork.

Supersnipe represented the imagined alter ego of Koppy McFad, known as the boy with the most comic books in the world. McFad immersed himself in countless comic books, allowing his imagination to transform him into a costumed superhero. He performs his superhero escapades reminiscent of Don Quixote, irritating both his family and his neighbors. Although he lacks any superhuman abilities, he can soar through the skies by filling his suit with helium.

There is no doubt that *The Great Gildersleeve* is not merely a relic of the past but an enduring symbol of laughter, community, and good-hearted resilience that lingers on in the hearts of many. The warmth and nostalgia of this beloved radio program reminds us of simpler times, ensuring that its heartwarming tales of home and family will continue to resonate with new generations. This is particularly relevant in the swiftly changing world of today, where division and the constant shifting of socio-political landscapes have led to concerns about the future and a yearning for the past.

lxi. *The Great Gildersleeve comic book story. Circa 1944.*

Appendix

Episode Logs

Fibber McGee and Molly

(Note:) Molly is absent from the program until April 18, 1939.

1938	
11/15	MCGEE IN "DR. JEKYLL AND MR. HYDE"
11/22	THE SURPRISE PARTY
11/29	MASQUERADE PARTY
12/06	HUNTING IN WYOMING
12/13	MANAGER MCGEE SELLS THE HOTEL
12/20	A CHRISTMAS GIFT FOR MCGEE'S NEPHEW
12/27	ACTING MAYOR MCGEE

1939	
1/03	MCGEE'S SHOOTING PAINS
1/10	MCGEE THE FIREMAN
1/17	MCGEE HAS INSOMNIA
1/24	MISSING SHIRT COLLAR BUTTON (*LAST SHOW FROM CHICAGO*)
1/31	MILITARY ADVISOR FOR ARMY MANEUVERS (*FIRST SHOW FROM HOLLYWOOD*)
2/07	FAULTY WINDOW SHADE
2/14	OUT OF COAL AND FROZEN WATER PIPES
2/21	AFTER DINNER SPEAKER AT ROTOWANTIS
2/28	MOUSE IN THE HOUSE
3/07	MCGEE'S HAMBURGER JOINT
3/14	THE GILDERSLEEVE MEMORY COURSE
3/21	THE SPRING HAIRCUT - DR. HARRY STORER
3/28	INHERITED YACHT
4/04	ANTIQUE FURNITURE
4/11	THE MAILMAN

4/18	MOLLY RETURNS - SETS UP BUDGET
4/25	MCGEE GETS GLASSES (DR. GILDERSLEEVE)
5/02	MCGEE DRIVES THE USED CAR HOME
5/09	DECIDING TO GO TO THE WORLD'S FAIR
5/16	ZITHER LESSONS & BURIED TREASURE
5/23	THE STORK
5/30	ESCAPED CONVICTS
6/06	MCGEE THE WRESTLER
6/13	ADVICE COLUMN - AUNT MOLLY & UNCLE FIBBER
6/20	TOOTHACHE (DR. GILDERSLEEVE)
6/27	THE LENDAHAND LOAN COMPANY
	SUMMER BREAK
9/05	MCGEE'S FISH FRY
9/12	15TH ANNIVERSARY - ELOPEMENT
9/19	NEWSPAPER COLUMN
9/26	FIBBER IS TOO SICK FOR HOUSEWORK
10/03	KILLER CANOVA'S AUTOGRAPH (*FIRST SHOW WITH THROCKMORTON P. GILDERSLEEVE*)
10/10	RUMMAGE SALE - BAZAAR
10/17	RAKING LEAVES
10/24	HALLOWEEN PARTY AT GILDERSLEEVE'S HOUSE
10/31	AUTO SHOW
11/07	HIAWATHA
11/14	TRAFFIC TICKET
11/21	OVERDUE LIBRARY BOOK
11/28	FINANCE COMPANY IS AFTER THE CAR
12/05	MCGEES ARE ADJUSTERS AT BONTON DEPARTMENT STORE
12/12	JEWELRY STORE ROBBERY
12/19	PACKAGE FROM UNCLE SYCAMORE ARRIVES
12/26	BUTLER GILDERSLEEVE

1940

1/02	MCGEE BUILDS A DOG HOUSE
1/09	GONE WITH THE WIND
1/16	NEW LICENSE PLATES - STOLEN CAR
1/23	GILDERSLEEVE GIRDLE SHOW
1/30	FIBBER TRIES TO GET RID OF AN OLD SUIT
2/06	FIBBER'S BIRTHDAY
2/13	EGYPTIAN GOOD LUCK RING
2/20	FIBBER HAS TO TELL THE TRUTH FOR AN HOUR
2/27	FIBBER IS CATCHING A COLD
3/05	CLEANING FIBBER'S CLOSET
3/12	MAKE A PAL OF YOUR WIFE WEEK
3/19	DOG LICENSE
3/26	PLANTING A HEDGE (PROPERTY LINE DISPUTE WITH GILDERSLEEVE)
4/02	WATCHING GILDY'S HOUSE
4/09	COMING HOME AFTER DOING "LUX RADIO THEATER"
4/16	5TH ANNIVERSARY SHOW FOR JOHNSON'S WAX
4/23	ART MUSEUM - HOW TO HANG A PICTURE
4/30	FIBBER THE DIRECTOR
5/07	WOMEN'S CLUB PLAY - STUCK IN SUIT OF ARMOR
5/14	MCGEE SPRAYS GILDY WITH GARDEN HOSE
5/21	MCGEES MIND PLUMBERS HARDWARE STORE
5/28	THE CIRCUS
6/04	SPAGHETTI DINNER FOR STAG PARTY
6/11	WALL PAPER
6/18	FIBBER MODELS A DRESS
6/25	PACKING FOR VACATION
	SUMMER BREAK
10/01	BACK FROM VACATION - UNPACKING

10/08	FIBBER QUITS SMOKING
10/15	FIBBER NEEDS A SCREWDRIVER
10/22	FIBBER FINDS GILDERSLEEVE'S LOCKED DIARY
10/29	TRIP TO NOTRE DAME/ARMY FOOTBALL GAME
11/05	ELECTION OFFICIALS
11/12	FIBBER'S BLACK EYE
11/19	TRAIN TRIP TO SEE UNCLE DENNIS
11/26	UNCLE DENNIS VISITS THE MCGEES
12/03	RAFFLE TICKET - FIVE TONS OF COAL
12/10	MAILING CHRISTMAS PACKAGES
12/17	GILDERSLEEVE FOR PRESIDENT
12/24	THE RADIO - PHONOGRAPH
12/31	FIBBER FINDS A WATCH AT 14TH & OAK

OTHER APPEARANCES	
5/27/41	GILDY'S LADDER - FIBBER MAKES A RECORD
9/30/41	BACK FROM VACATION - GILDY SAYS GOODBYE
12/23/41	CHRISTMAS PRESENTS *(GILDERSLEEVE COMES TO VISIT)*
4/04/44	FIBBER THE CONVALESCENT *(GILDERSLEEVE ASSUMED THE LEAD ROLE WHILE JIM WAS IN THE HOSPITAL.)*

lxii. The two Gildersleeves, Willard Waterman and Harold Peary, backstage at *A Funny Thing Happened on the Way to the Forum.* Courtesy of Mary Anna Waterman.

The Great Gildersleeve

	1941
5/14	AUDITION SHOW
	SERIES PREMIERE
8/31	ARRIVES AT SUMMERFIELD
9/07	BIRDIE ARRIVES
9/14	LEROY'S PAPER ROUTE
9/21	MARJORIE'S GIRLFRIEND VISITS
9/28	HICCUPS
10/05	INVESTIGATE THE CITY JAIL
10/12	MISSING EPISODE
10/19	PRANKS AT SCHOOL
10/26	A VISIT FROM OLIVER
11/02	BABY SITTING
11/09	BIRDIE QUITS
11/16	SERVICEMAN FOR THANKSGIVING
11/23	LEROY SMOKES A CIGAR
11/30	THE CANARY WON'T SING
12/07	COUSIN OCTAVIA VISITS
12/14	SELLING THE IRON DEER
12/21	CHRISTMAS GIFT FOR FIBBER
12/28	LEROY'S NEW DOG

	1942
1/04	GILDY GOES ON A DIET
1/11	GILDY ARRESTED AS CAR THIEF
1/18	A NEW BED FOR MARJORIE
1/25	MATCHMAKER
2/01	LEROY RUNS AWAY
2/08	AUTO MECHANICS
2/15	GILDY'S SUIT IS AT A CHINESE LAUNDRY
2/22	SELLING THE DRUGSTORE
3/01	FORTUNE TELLER
3/08	WAR STAMPS LEFT IN DONATED BOOK
3/15	TEN BEST-DRESSED
3/22	GILDY'S NEW NEIGHBORS
3/29	GILDY WRITES TO SERVICEMEN FOR MARJORIE

4/06	EASTER EGG HUNT	
4/13	BLACKOUT WARDEN	
4/20	LEROY SELLS FLOWER SEEDS	
4/26	GILDY'S GOAT HORACE	
5/03	SHIP CHRISTENING	
5/10	MYSTERY VOICE	
5/17	COLLEGE CHUM VISITS	
5/24	GILDY HAS THREE DATES FOR A DANCE	
5/31	TESTIMONIAL DINNER FOR JUDGE HOOKER	
6/07	THE SNEEZES	
6/14	GILDY PRODUCES A PLAY	
6/21	FATHER'S DAY CHAIR	
6/28	GILDY IS IN LOVE WITH AMELIA	
	SUMMER BREAK	
8/30	FISHING TRIP TO LAKE HACKMASACK	
9/06	GOLF TOURNAMENT	
9/13	WINNING THE WAR	
9/20	MEET LEILA RANSOME	
9/27	COMPETITION FROM THE JUDGE	
10/04	PLANTING A TREE	
10/11	FIRST COLD SNAP	
10/18	APPOINTED WATER COMMISSIONER	
10/25	GILDY'S FIRST DAY ON THE JOB	
11/01	A PAL TO LEROY	
11/08	QUIET EVENING AT HOME	
11/15	COLLEGE CHUM'S SON VISITS	
11/22	THANKSGIVING DINNER	
11/29	ATTEND THE THEATRE - DATE WITH A STAR	
12/06	TOOTHACHE	
12/13	BIRDIE LEAVES TO VISIT RELATIVES	
12/20	CHRISTMAS PROGRAM	
12/27	LEROY'S CHEMISTRY SET	

	1943	
1/03	WANTING TO MARRY LEILA	
1/10	FIBBER MCGEE & MOLLY VISIT	
1/17	WOMEN'S CLUB SPEAKER	
1/24	SABOTAGE	
1/31	FIRE ENGINE COMMITTEE	
2/07	LEILA'S SISTER	
2/14	LEROY SENDS PRANK VALENTINES	
2/21	GILDY IS INVITED TO JOIN THE KEYSTONE CLUB	
2/28	BIRTHDAY DINNER FOR JUDGE HOOKER	
3/07	GILDY DIETS AGAIN	
3/14	INCOME TAX TIME	
3/21	COMMUNITY VICTORY GARDEN	
3/28	SPRINGTIME IN SUMMERFIELD	
4/04	GILDY REPAIRS HIS CAR	
4/11	AUTO ACCIDENT WITH JUDGE HOOKER	
4/18	SPRING HIKE	
4/25	RABBITS	
5/02	HARD WATER	
5/09	WEDDING LIST	
5/16	HAUNTED HOUSE	
5/23	LEROY GETS A JOB	
5/30	MEMORIAL DAY PARADE	
6/06	WEDDING SHOWER FOR LEILA	
6/13	GILDY PLANS HONEYMOON	
6/20	BACHELOR DINNER FOR GILDY	
6/27	WEDDING DAY	
	SUMMER BREAK	
8/29	END OF VACATION AT GRASS LAKE	
9/05	NEW GRAMMAR SCHOOL PRINCIPAL	
9/12	WAR BOND DRIVE	
9/19	LEILA RETURNING	
9/26	LEILA ARRIVES HOME	
10/03	AFTER SCHOOL ACTIVITIES	
10/10	ROYAL VISIT	
10/17	HEART TROUBLE	
10/24	LOW WATER PRESSURE	
10/31	HALLOWEEN PARTY	
11/07	THE POT ROAST	

11/14	GILDY REJECTED BY EVE GOODWIN
11/21	MOOSE HUNT
11/28	CONCERT PIANIST HOUSE GUEST
12/05	COLLECTING AN UNPAID WATER BILL
12/12	MARJORIE RUNS AWAY
12/19	CHRISTMAS EVE SEARCH PARTY
12/26	RAINY DAY AFTER CHRISTMAS
1944	
1/02	NEW YEAR, NEW MAN
1/09	GILDY IN HOSPITAL
1/16	INCOME TAX RETURNS
1/23	EVE AND GILDY GET TOGETHER
1/30	MARJORIE THE ACTRESS
2/06	SLEIGH RIDE
2/13	ANONYMOUS VALENTINE FOR GILDY
2/20	GILDY MEETS BRUCE FAIRFIELD
2/27	GILDY TO PLAY CYRANO
3/05	BALANCING THE CHECKBOOK
3/12	TESTING THE POLITICAL WATERS
3/19	GILDY WANTS TO RUN FOR MAYOR
3/26	EXERCISING FOR CAMPAIGN BUTTON PHOTO
4/2	PLANNING ELECTION PLATFORM
4/9	CAMPAIGN OFFICIALLY STARTS - EASTER SHOW
4/16	ESCORTING TWO WOMEN ON EASTER MORNING
4/23	ARBOR DAY SPEAKER
4/30	ENGAGED
5/07	CAMPAIGN GETS HOT
5/14	GILDY ENGAGED TO EVE, BUT KISSES LEILA
5/21	CITY EMPLOYEES PICNIC
5/28	CAMPAIGN HEADQUARTERS
6/04	EVE'S MOTHER VISITS
6/11	DINNER FOR EVE'S MOTHER
6/18	EVE'S MOTHER STAYS ON
6/25	ELECTION DAY - GILDY LOSES
	SUMMER BREAK

9/03	THE NEED FOR HUMAN COMPANIONSHIP
9/10	WATER COMMISSIONER IS FIRED - RAIN MAKER
9/17	MCGEE'S INVENTION
9/24	PLASTIC MOUSE TRAP - BANKER'S SON
10/01	GILDY SELLS HIS HOUSE
10/08	BOY'S CLUB
10/15	GILDY LOOKS FOR A JOB
10/22	IMPORTANT PHONE CALL
10/29	GILDY BACK AS WATER COMMISSIONER
11/05	ELECTION DAY - BET
11/12	THE SPANISH DANCER
11/19	RECEPTION FOR MISS DEL REY
11/26	RECEPTION AFTERMATH
12/03	A DATE WITH MISS DEL RAY
12/10	BREACH OF PROMISE
12/17	SHADOWING
12/24	TWAS THE NIGHT BEFORE CHRISTMAS
12/31	BIG NEW YEAR'S EVE PARTY

	1945
1/07	WHO'S DATING WHO
1/14	ENGAGEMENT FOR THE DEFENSE
1/21	THE HOCKEY PLAYER
1/28	AUNT HATTIE IS DUE TO ARRIVE
2/04	VISIT BY AUNT HATTIE
2/11	AUNT HATTIE TAKES OVER
2/18	AUNT HATTIE STAYS ON
2/25	HATTIE AND HOOKER
3/04	HIDING FROM HATTIE
3/11	CHAIRMAN OF WOMEN'S COMMITTEE
3/18	LEILA HEARS A BURGLAR
3/25	OLD FLAME NAMED VIOLET
4/01	RAISING A PIG
4/08	LEROY'S PET PIG TIGER
4/15	*PRE-EMPTED FOR FDR DEATH COVERAGE*
4/22	LEILA'S PARTY
4/29	NEW NEIGHBOR - BULLARD
5/06	GILDY PICKS A HUSBAND FOR MARJORIE

5/13	MEET CRAIG BULLARD
5/20	UNCLAIMED SAVINGS ACCOUNT - BUY STOCK
5/27	BESSIE QUITS
6/03	NEW SECRETARY - LEILA
6/10	AN EVENING WITH A GOOD BOOK
6/17	BULLARDS HAVE A PARTY
	SUMMER BREAK
9/02	GOING TO GRASS LAKE
9/09	LEROY'S NEW TEACHER
9/16	LEROY SUSPENDED FROM SCHOOL
9/23	LEILA RETURNS HOME
9/30	MARJORIE THE BALLERINA
10/07	RAKING LEAVES - CRAIG'S PARTY
10/14	LEROY WORKS OFF A BROKEN VASE
10/21	LIGHTFOOT VISITS LEILA
10/28	PEAVEY'S WIFE IS ILL - RUMOR
11/04	HELPING LEROY WITH HIS STUDIES
11/11	TEACHING MARJORIE DOMESTIC ARTS
11/18	FALLING OUT OF THE JOLLY BOYS
11/25	BIG FOOTBALL GAME
12/02	GILDY STUCK WITH OPERA TICKETS
12/09	GILDY HEAD OF OPERA COMMITTEE
12/16	A NIGHT AT THE OPERA
12/23	CHRISTMAS EVE AT HOME
12/30	NEW YEAR'S EVE AT HOME

	1946
1/06	BEN RETURNS FROM THE NAVY
1/13	BEN SELLS LIFE INSURANCE
1/20	EXPOSING A PHONY SWAMI
1/27	GILDY AND LEILA FEEL THEIR AGE
2/03	FEUD WITH THE BULLARDS - DIPLOMAT GILDY
2/10	NEED A NEW CAR
2/17	LEROY HAS THE FLU
2/24	GILDY'S NEW HOBBY - BOAT IN A BOTTLE
3/03	STATE WATER INSPECTOR

3/10	MARJORIE'S DANCE DATE WITH UNCLE MORT	
3/17	LEROY AND CRAIG ARRESTED	
3/24	GILDY TRACES GENEALOGY	
3/31	PICNIC BEFORE DOOMSDAY	
4/07	ANNUAL DINNER WITH JUDGE HOOKER	
4/14	BANK ROBBER LOOSE	
4/21	PETITION AGAINST TROLLEY CAR HOUSE	
4/28	LEROY WANTS A PONY	
5/05	GILDY IN A RUT - NEW IMAGE	
5/12	LEILA'S NEW BOY FRIEND	
5/19	LEROY LEARNS TO DANCE - PARTY FOR ETHEL	
5/26	FLASHBACK - MEETS LEILA RANSOME	
6/02	FLASHBACK - PLAYS CYRANO, MEET EVE	
6/09	FLASHBACK - JOLLY BOYS 4TH OF JULY PICNIC	
	SUMMER BREAK	
9/18	THE COMMISSIONER TURNS OFF THE WATER	
9/25	GILDY'S NEW SPRUCE SCENT - LEILA ENGAGED	
10/02	LEILA'S WEDDING INVITATIONS	
10/09	LEILA LEAVES TOWN	
10/16	GILDY CONTEMPLATES EARLY RETIREMENT	
10/23	GILDY ASKS FOR A RAISE	
10/20	REAL ESTATE AGENT - HOOKER AS A BOARDER	
11/06	PAJAMA PARTY - MARJORIE GETS ENGAGED	
11/13	SMITTEN BY AN UNKNOWN BEAUTIFUL LADY	
11/20	GILDY TAKES UP THE GREAT BOOKS	
11/27	BIRDY TAKES A VACATION	
12/04	JOLLY BOYS SPONSOR AN ORPHAN	
12/11	LEROY AFRAID OF A BULLY	
12/18	LEROY WANTS A MOTOR SCOOTER	
12/25	CHRISTMAS CAROLING	

	1947
1/01	BIG NEW YEAR'S COSTUME BALL
1/08	LEILA BACK FOR A VISIT - GILDY IN LOVE
1/15	JOLLY BOY'S SLEIGHRIDE - JUDGE HOOKER ILL
1/22	DANCING SCHOOL
1/29	MARJORIE'S HOTROD BOYFRIEND
2/05	MAGAZINE SALESMAN
2/12	OLD SCHOOL FRIEND VISITS GILDY
2/19	BESSIE'S COUSIN SUBSTITUTES FOR HER
2/26	GETTING RID OF BESSIE
3/05	MARJORIE FLIPPED OVER CROONER LARRY LAKE
3/12	LEROY AND CRAIG PICKED UP TAKING LUMBER
3/19	STUCK WITH WATER DEPARTMENT MONEY OVER NIGHT
3/26	FIRST DAY OF SPRING - NEW PIANO TEACHER
4/02	EVENING WITH MISS PIPER
4/09	BIRD WATCHERS
4/16	THE WHOLE WORLD IS WATCHING
4/23	LEILA'S PARTY FOR JOANNE
4/30	THE GREAT TCHAIKOWSKY LOVE STORY
5/07	LEROY EXCLUDED FROM CRAIG'S PARTY
5/14	PEAVY DISAPPEARS
5/21	TEACHER'S PROBLEMS
5/28	GILDY TRIES TO GIVE UP SMOKING
6/04	CALLED IN BY THE I.R.S.
	SUMMER BREAK
9/10	GILDY TRIES TO RENEW ROMANCE WITH EVE
9/17	GETTING EVERYTHING SNUG FOR WINTER
9/24	IN TROUBLE WITH BESSIE'S BOY FRIEND
10/01	TEACHING LEROY BORROWING AND FINANCE
10/08	BEAUTIFUL VISITOR AT THE BULLARDS

10/15	MARJORIE'S BABY TENDING ASSIGNMENT
10/22	CONGRESSMAN GUILDERSLEEVE
10/29	HALLOWEEN PARTY
11/05	HAYRIDE
11/12	GILDY SWINDLED ON A FUR COAT
11/19	LEROY IN SCHOOL PLAY
11/26	THANKSGIVING - TOM SAWYER RAFT
12/03	FISCAL REPORT DUE
12/10	CHRISTMAS SHOPPING
12/17	WATER COMMISSIONER ACCUSED OF LOAFING
12/24	LEROY'S CHRISTMAS DOG
12/31	NEW YEAR'S EVE PARTIES

1948

1/07	ANNE TUTTLE IS BACK IN TOWN
1/14	GILDY ENCOURAGES MARJORIE'S NEW ROMANCE
1/21	SCHOOL BOARD ELECTION GILDY VS. HOOKER
1/28	LICENSE PLATE TIME/ BARBER SHOP TRIP
2/04	ACTING MAYOR
2/11	GETTING GLASSES
2/18	LEILAS COUSIN ADELINE FAIRCHILD ARRIVES
2/25	GILDY THINKS ADELINE IS STEALING BIRDIE
3/03	GILDY HELPS GIRL - SHY LEROY
3/10	GILDY CONSIDERS MARRIAGE
3/17	ADELINES BEAU CECIL
3/24	ADELINE WANTS TO VISIT THE JOLLY BOYS
3/31	MARJORIE IN LOVE WITH HER FRENCH TEACHER
4/07	GILDY RAISING MONEY FOR BASEBALL FIELD
4/14	THE WATER COMMISSIONER'S RADIO SPEECH

4/21	GILDY'S NEW SECRETARY	
4/28	DINNER COURTESY OF HERCULES KITCHENWARE	
5/05	FISH FRY	
5/12	GILDY STAYS HOME SICK	
5/19	GREEN THUMB WOMEN'S CLUB	
5/26	GILDY DRIVES A MERCEDES	
6/02	GILDY FIRED AS WATER COMMISSIONER	
	SUMMER BREAK	
9/08	BABY GIRL LEFT IN GILDY'S CAR	
9/15	TAKING CARE OF BABY	
9/22	TAKING PICTURES OF BABY UPSETS LEROY	
9/29	NAME THE BABY CONTEST	
10/06	GILDY TRIES TO REFORM FOR WELFARE INVESTIGATOR	
10/13	VISIT BY AUNT HATTIE	
10/20	MARJORIE READY TO MARRY TO KEEP BABY	
10/27	GILDY PROPOSES TO ADELINE	
11/03	SECRET ENGAGEMENT	
11/10	LEILA RANSOME BACK IN TOWN	
11/17	ENGAGED TO LEILA AND ADELINE	
11/24	WATER COMMISSIONER'S HELICOPTER FLIGHT	
12/01	LEROY'S HOLIDAY JOB	
12/08	DISAPPEARING CHRISTMAS GIFTS	
12/15	ECONOMY FOR CHRISTMAS	
12/22	CHRISTMAS EVE AT GILDERSLEEVE'S	
12/29	A WEDDING IS IMMINENT	

	1949
1/05	GILDY TAKES UP WRITING
1/12	LOVE THY NEIGHBOR
1/19	TRIP TO THE DENTIST
1/26	EAGER YOUNG MAN AT THE WATER DEPARTMENT
2/02	ADELINE'S HAT SHOP
2/09	HAT SHOP GRAND OPENING
2/16	LEILA ARRIVES TO CLOSE THE HAT SHOP

2/23	SINGING LESSONS
3/02	LEROY'S GIRL-FRIEND AND HER MOTHER
3/09	GILDY'S DREAM - SUMMERFIELD 1903
3/16	LEROY FACES COMPETITION
3/23	GILDY'S NEW SECRETARY
3/30	ACTING POLICE COMMISSIONER
4/06	THE BABY'S BIRTHDAY PARTY CONFLICTS
4/13	THE CIRCUS COMES TO SUMMERFIELD
4/20	HAUNTED HOUSE
4/27	DETECTIVE GILDERSLEEVE AFTER BURGLAR
5/04	MYSTERIOUS GIRL ON THE BUS
5/11	GILDY'S MILLIONAIRE FRIEND VISITS
5/18	MARJORIE AND RODNEY, THE POET
5/25	GILDY SUES BULLARD
6/01	FOLK DANCING CLASS
	SUMMER BREAK
9/21	SONGWRITER
9/28	GILDY'S NEW HEARTHROB: NURSE MILFORD
10/05	DOUBLE DATE WITH MARJORIE AND BRONCO
10/12	GILDY AT HOSPITAL WITH EXPECTANT FATHER
10/19	TOM CAT TROUBLES
10/26	GILDY'S RIVEL, DR. OLSON
11/02	RIVALRY CONTINUES AT THE CARNIVAL
11/09	BIRTHDAY TEA PARTY FOR MARJORIE
11/16	A JOB FOR BRONCO
11/23	THE JOLLY BOYS BAND
11/30	NEW NEIGHBOR - TWO PANTS PEARSON
12/07	BRONCO BOWS OUT FOR MARSHALL BULLARD
12/14	THE CHRISTMAS SPIRIT
12/21	MARJORIE AND BRONCO ARE ENGAGED
12/28	HAYRIDE

1950

1/04	ENGAGEMENT ANNOUNCEMENT - BRONCO'S FAMILY
1/11	YOUNG FRENCH D.P. COMES TO SUMMERFIELD
1/18	DINNER WITH KATHRYN
1/25	DINNER FOR BRONCO'S FOLKS
2/01	GILDY TRIES TO LEARN THE SAMBA
2/08	SHOULD MARJORIE WORK AFTER MARRIAGE
2/15	WEDDING DAY SET FOR MARJORIE & BRONCO
2/22	JOLLY BOY ELECTION
3/01	MARJORIE'S SHOWER
3/08	GILDY'S BLADE
3/15	GILDY CONSIDERS MARRIAGE
3/22	PICNIC WITH THE THOMPSONS
3/29	HOUSE GUEST - JUDGE HOOKER
4/05	APPARTMENT FOR BRONCO & MARJORIE
4/12	LEROY'S BILLY GOAT
4/19	MARJORIE'S WEDDING GOWN
4/26	JOLLY BOYS GIFT - A RENTAL TRAILER
5/03	BRONCO DISAPPEARS
5/10	WEDDING DAY
5/17	FISHING TRIP TO GRASS LAKE
5/24	BRONCO THE REAL ESTATE SALESMAN
5/31	SADIE HAWKINS DAY DANCE
6/07	HOUSE BOAT
6/14	VACATION PLANS ON THE HOUSE BOAT *(LAST SHOW WITH HAROLD PEARY)*
	SUMMER BREAK
9/06	MARJORIE IS PREGNANT *(FIRST SHOW WITH WILLARD WATERMAN)*
9/13	VISITING IN-LAWS - MRS.THOMPSON'S SISTER
9/20	GILDY LOOKING FOR NEW SECRETARY
9/27	GILDY SHARES LEROY'S PIANO LESSONS
10/04	COMMUNITY CHEST FOOTBALL GAME
10/11	BULLARD RUNS FOR MAYOR
10/18	WEIGHT PROBLEMS

10/25	THE SONS OF SUMMERFIELD	
11/01	ELECTION DAY	
11/08	A BETTER MAN THAN BULLARD	
11/15	SUMMERFIELD CENTENNIAL PAGEANT	
11/22	WATER DEPARTMENT CALENDAR	
11/29	LEROY'S FIRST DATE	
12/06	LEROY'S LAUNDRY BUSINESS	
12/13	CHIEF GATES ON THE SPOT	
12/20	CHRISTMAS SHOW - A PRESENT FOR KATHRYN	
12/27	GILDY-BULLARD DOUBLE DATE NEW YEAR'S EVE	

	1951
1/03	MARJORIE CRAVES SAUERKRAUT
1/10	GILDY IS WORN OUT FROM LATE DATING
1/17	A NERVOUS EXPECTANT FATHER
1/31	A SHOWER FOR MARJORIE
2/07	DAY OFF FOR PEAVEY
2/14	THROWING SNOWBALLS
2/21	MARJORIE'S BABIES ARRIVE
2/28	TRYING TO NAME THE TWINS
3/07	MARJORIE AND THE TWINS COMING HOME
3/14	GILDY PUSHES ATTENDANCE AT THE JOLLY BOYS CLUB
3/21	BRONCO TRIES TO RUN THE HOUSE
3/28	GILDY AND LEROY BABY SIT THE TWINS
4/04	BULLARD NEEDS BOAT ACCESS
4/11	GILDY WORRIED THAT KIDS WANT TO LEAVE
4/18	LEROY IN LOVE WITH MARCELLE
4/25	LEROY'S PONY
5/02	SPRING CLEANING THE JUDGE'S HOUSE
5/09	MARJORIE AND BRONCO'S FIRST ANNIVERSARY
5/16	BOATING DATE WITH KATHARINE
5/23	BRONCO'S FATHER ARRIVES
5/30	LEAVING ON VACATION TO HALF MOON LAKE

	SUMMER BREAK
9/05	LEROY BUYS A CAR
9/12	COUNTY FAIR COMES TO SUMMERFIELD
9/19	GETTING READY FOR SCHOOL - WOMEN TROUBLE
9/26	MARJORIE GETS A JOB
10/03	GILDY WANTS TO BE RE-ELECTED PRESIDENT OF THE JOLLY BOYS CLUB
10/10	LEROY VISITS THE JUDGE
10/17	BRONCO ALMOST FORGETS ABOUT HIS FIRST DATE WITH MARJORIE
10/24	GILDY TAKES MRS. WINTHROP AND BABS ON A PICNIC
10/31	HALLOWEEN AND GILDY FINDS A LOST BOY
11/07	MARJORIE AND BRONCO WANT TO BUILD A HOUSE
11/14	MARJORIE AND BRONCO DECIDE WHICH LOT TO BUY
11/21	INVITING THANKSGIVING GUESTS
11/28	GETTING LEROY TO STUDY
12/05	MISSING EPISODE
12/12	LEROY SELLING CHRISTMAS TREES
12/19	CHRISTMAS SHOW
12/26	OPENING LAST CHRISTMAS PRESENTS

	1952
1/02	GILDY WANTS NEW JOB TO KEEP UP WITH BRONCO
1/09	GILDY HAS DISAPPEARED IN THE HOSPITAL
1/16	GILDY TALKS TO EVERYONE ABOUT OPERSTION
1/23	TRYING TO BE ALONE WITH PAULA
1/30	GILDY PROTECTS HOOKER FROM MONA
2/06	GILDY HIRES MRS. MUNSON
2/13	ENGAGEMENT RING MIXUP
2/20	CIVIC COORDINATOR
2/27	LEROY'S WEEK OF FREEDOM
3/05	BULLARD IS HOUSE GUEST

3/12	TRAIN TRIP TO OMAHA
3/19	GILDY'S GARDEN
3/26	TELEVISION COMES TO SUMMERFIELD
4/02	COLORFUL PAST
4/09	EASTER SUNRISE SERVICE
4/16	LEROY THE BEE KEEPER
4/23	DIVING FOR PUBLICITY
4/30	BAD REPORT CARD - NO CAMP
5/07	LEROY THE SINGING COWBOY
5/14	BRONCO COMING HOME
5/21	HAPPY MOVING DAY
5/28	LEROY'S BIKE MOTOR
6/04	KATIE LEE VISITS SUMMERFIELD
6/11	BRONCO WANTS A WALL BETWEEN YARDS
6/18	GUESS THE NUMBER OF BEANS CONTEST
6/25	MISS MCKINLEY OF THE COMPLAINT DEPARTMENT
7/02	FOURTH OF JULY SPEECH
7/09	FISHING WITH MISS MCKINLEY
7/16	BACK YARD CAMPING
7/23	SUGGESTION BOX
7/30	BRONCO SELLS GILDY'S HOUSE
8/06	LEROY BEHAVING TOO WELL
8/13	GILDY GOES ON A DIET
8/20	LEROY'S MILLION DOLLAR LAUNDRY
8/27	COUSIN EMILY COMES FOR A VISIT
9/03	WINNING LEROY BACK FROM EMILY
9/10	CLEANING BULLARD'S HOUSE
9/17	DRIVER'S LICENSE TEST
9/25	HOOKER AND PEAVEY ARE FEUDING
10/01	ECONOMIZE
10/08	LADIE'S MAN
10/15	WATCH TROUBLE
10/22	GILDY THE ATHLETE
10/29	THE HAUNTED HOUSE
11/05	GILDERSLEEVE VS. GOLF
11/12	PROBLEMS WITH LEROY'S TEACHER
11/19	LEROY'S GIFT

11/26	MISS GRACE TUTTLE AND BIRD WATCHING
12/03	THE BIRTHDAY DUCK DINNER
12/10	LEROY'S PART TIME EMPLOYMENT
12/17	GRACE TUTTLE'S BROTHER SYDNEY
12/24	GILDY AND LEROY ALONE FOR CHRISTMAS
12/31	NEW YEAR'S EVE WITH PEAVEY

1953	
1/07	LEILA BACK IN TOWN - SIDNEY TUTTLE
1/14	GILDY AND SIDNEY HELP LEILA
1/21	UNCLE BERT SENDS LEROY A GREAT DANE
1/28	GILDY AND GRACE TUTTLE
2/04	RIVALS, LEILA & GRACE, MEET
2/11	TWO DATES FOR MAYOR'S VALENTINE PARTY
2/18	GILDY IN TROUBLE WITH LEILA & GRACE
2/25	GILDY'S GREAT DANE CAUSES PEAVEY TROUBLE
3/04	EXTRA HELP AT THE WATER DEPARTMENT
3/11	LEROY MOVES OUT TO MARJORIE'S
3/18	THE JAM SESSION
3/25	CLEANING THE HOUSE – RUMMAGE SALE
4/01	EASTER SUNRISE SERVICE
4/08	LEROY HAS TROUBLE WITH THE MAYOR'S SON
4/15	BOY'S CLUB TAKES OVER JOLLY BOYS CLUBROOM
4/22	MARJORIE AND BRONCO ARE FIGHTING
4/29	BOTTLED WATER COMPANY STOCK
5/06	ANNIVERSARY PRESENT
5/13	GILDY GOING TO EUROPE?
5/20	LEROY'S THEME
5/27	WITNESS AT THE WEDDING
6/03	BIRDIE MAY MOVE TO MARJORIE'S HOUSE

6/10	LEROY HAS THE MUMPS - TRAIN STOP
6/17	GIFT FOR MISS TUTTLE
6/24	SWIMMING TRIP TO GRASS LAKE
7/01	TOGETHERNESS
7/08	KATIE LEE RETURNS
7/15	BUYING A SPRAY GUN
7/22	MAE HOME FROM VACATION- ENGAGED
7/29	LEROY GOING TO VISIT AUNT HATTIE
8/05	THE WATER COMMISSIONER IS FIRED
8/12	DECIDING ON A LAKE CABIN
8/19	A FISH STORY
8/26	SUFFICIENT UNTO ONE'S SELF
9/02	LEROY'S GIRL - JO MAC
9/09	GILDY HELPS RAISE RONNIE
9/16	BIRDIE'S MYSTERY CAKE RECIPE
9/23	BABY SITTER GILDY
9/30	FLATTERY
10/07	HOME HAIRCUT
10/14	GILDY INVOLVED WITH TEACHER & PRINCIPAL
10/21	FIRE BELLS ARE RINGING
10/28	UNWILLING WITNESS
11/04	IMPULSIVE GILDY ALMOST GETS MARRIED
11/11	THE AUTHORITY FIGURE
11/18	GILDY THE ATHLETE VS. DOC OLSEN
11/25	DINNER MIXUP WITH PEAVEY & GIRLS
12/02	GILDY EARNS CHRISTMAS MONEY SELLING INSURANCE
12/09	TAKING BESSIE TO THE DANCE
12/16	GILDY & HOOKER FEUD AT CHRISTMAS
12/23	SELLING TREES FOR NEEDY CHILDREN'S PARTY
12/30	NEW YEAR'S EVE AT HOME WITH LEROY

	1954
1/06	IRENE'S FATHER PUSHES FOR A WEDDING
1/13	GILDY IN THE DOGHOUSE WITH IRENE
1/20	LEROY GOING STEADY
1/27	BRONCO MAD AT GILDY FOR INTERFERRING
2/03	EVENING CONFERENCE WITH LEROY'S TEACHER
2/10	JUDGE HOOKER'S ANNUAL DINNER
2/17	GILDY THE BUDDING POLITICIAN
2/24	JOLLY BOYS' ELECTION
3/03	PAULA WINTHROP BACK IN TOWN
3/10	GILDY IS OLD FASHIONED AND SQUARE
3/17	NEW GIRL IN TOWN - MARIE OLSEN
3/24	HOBBY SHOW
3/31	GILDY INVOLVED WITH TWO GIRLS AGAIN
4/07	MARIE TEACHES BRONCO FRENCH
4/14	DINNER PARTY FOR BRONCO'S BOSS
4/21	MARIE OLSEN CHARMS EVERYONE
4/28	GILDY SWEARS OFF GIRLS, BUT MEETS THELMA
5/05	MISSING EPISODE
5/12	DINNER FOR DR. OLSEN WHO'S LEAVING TOWN
5/19	GILDY RUNS FOR SHERIFF
5/26	VISIT BY AUNT HATTIE
6/02	TRYING TO END AUNT HATTIE'S STAY

1955	
10/20	FLOYD'S INHEARITANCE
10/27-12/29	MISSING EPISODES

1956	
1/05	FIBBING TO MAKE FRIENDS
1/15-1/19	MISSING EPISODES
1/26	LEAP YEAR PARTY
2/02-10/25	MISSING EPISODES
11/01	JOLLY BOYS HAUNTED HOUSE ADVENTURE
11/08-12/27	MISSING EPISODES

1957	
1/03-2/28	MISSING EPISODES
3/07	SERIOUS CALAMITY
3/14-4/11	MISSING EPISODES
4/18	THE MEANING OF EASTER
10/17-12/26	MISSING EPISODES

1958	
1/02-3/27	MISSING EPISODES

The Harold Peary Show

	1950
8/23	AUDITION SHOW
	SERIES PREMIER
9/17	HAROLD LOSES HIS JOB AT THE RADIO STATION
9/24	PLAN TO RENAME BOOMER PARK
10/04	ADVERTISING SHARK REPELLENT POWDER ON THE RADIO SHOW
10/11	HAROLD FALLS FOR A CHANTEUSE
10/18	THE RUNAWAY BOY
10/25	HAROLD'S CAMPAIGN SPEECH
11/01	HAROLD DECIDES HE WANTS TO LOSE THE ELECTION
11/08	COUSIN RAYMOND VISITS
11/15	GETTING A JOB FOR RAYMOND
11/22	THANKSGIVING PLAY
12/06	HAROLD MEETS THE HUMMER
12/13	HAROLD HELPS RAYMOND AND GLORIA GO TO THE DANCE
12/20	SANTA AT THE CHILDREN'S CHRISTMAS PARTY
12/27	NEW YEAR'S BARN DANCE

	1951
1/03	MRS. O'DAY'S WARBLEWARE PARTY
1/10	HAROLD LOSES HIS SPONSOR AND TRIES A NEW SHOW
1/17	HAROLD THINKS OF GOING TO NEW YORK
1/24	HAROLD GETS ENGAGED - TWICE
1/31	CIVIC ACHIEVEMENT AWARD
2/07	HAROLD'S MOTHER HAS A SUITOR
2/14	MISTAKEN VALENTINES
2/21	FLORABELLE RETURNS
2/28	WILLIS CAN'T PASS THE PHYSICAL
3/07	RED CROSS DRIVE
3/14	INCOME TAX
3/21	COUSIN MARVIN COMES TO STAY

3/28	COUSIN MARVIN'S FIRST DAY OF SCHOOL
4/04	MODERNIZING DOC'S OFFICE
4/18	HAROLD DECIDES TO CLEAN OUT THE CELLAR
4/25	CIRCUS DAY
5/02	MARVIN'S GANG
5/09	HAROLD AND MR. WALKER VIE FOR CLASS
5/16	DOES FLORABELLE HAVE A NEW LOVER
5/23	MARVIN IS INVITED TO A PARTY
5/30	HAROLD IS MARSHALL FOR A DAY
6/06	PEABODY'S SISTER TAKES OVER THE RADIO STATION
6/13	MARVIN DECIDES TO STAY WITH HAROLD

Filmography

lxiii. Lobby card for the 1941 film Look Who's Laughing. Public domain.

Look Who's Laughing (1941)

Edgar Bergen and Charlie McCarthy are enlisted by Fibber McGee to convince an aircraft manufacturer to build a factory in the quaint town of Wistful Vista.

Cast

Edgar Bergen as himself

Charlie McCarthy as himself

Jim Jordan as Fibber McGee

Marian Jordan as Molly McGee

Harold Peary as Throckmorton P. Gildersleeve

Lucille Ball as Julie Patterson

Isabel Randolph as Abigail Uppington

Here We Go Again (1942)

It's Fibber and Molly's twentieth anniversary and they decide to throw a party. However, in the face of disappointment as each invitation is declined, they make the bold choice to embark on a second honeymoon instead. They journey back to the historic Ramble Inn where they hope to relive the cherished memories of their honeymoon. When they arrive, they unexpectedly reunite with their friends, Edgar Bergan, Charlie McCarthy, Gildersleeve, and Mrs. Uppington. The party is back on, and it's bound to be an experience they'll treasure forever. But here's the catch: how will Fibber manage to pay for all of this?

Cast

Jim Jordan as Fibber McGee

Marian Jordan as Molly

Edgar Bergen as himself

Charlie McCarthy as himself

Harold Peary as Throckmorton P. Gildersleeve

Gale Gordon as Otis Cadwalader

Ginny Simms as Jean Gildersleeve

Isabel Randolph as Abigail Uppington

Bill Thompson as Wallace Wimple

Seven Days' Leave (1942)

Soldier Johnny Grey finds himself entangled in a captivating tale of love and fortune. Just as he prepares to embark on a lifelong journey with the enchanting singer Mapy Cortes, fate intervenes with an unexpected twist. Johnny discovers that he is the rightful heir to a staggering $100,000 inheritance from his great-grandfather. However, there's a small condition attached to this incredible opportunity. Johnny is required to marry a descendant of his great-grandfather's Civil War rival, the renowned General Havelock-Allen.

Cast

Victor Mature as Johnny Grey

Lucille Ball as Terry Havelock-Allen

Harold Peary as Throckmorton P. Gildersleeve

Ginny Simms as herself

Les Brown as himself

Freddy Martin as himself

Arnold Stang as Bitsy

Buddy Clark as himself

Gildersleeve's Bad Day (1943)

The story centers on Summerfield's courthouse, where Gildersleeve fulfills his civic duty as a juror in a bank robbery trial, with the notorious Louie Barton (Douglas Fowley) as the accused. Without Gildersleeve's knowledge, he becomes the target of a bribe offer from the defendant. As the jury reaches a vote of 11-1 in favor of conviction, Gildersleeve emerges as the sole holdout.

Cast

Harold Peary as Throckmorton P. Gildersleeve

Jane Darwell as Aunt Emma

Nancy Gates as Margie Forrester

Charles Arnt as Judge Horace Hooker

Freddie Mercer as Leroy Forrester

Lillian Randolph as Birdie

Grant Withers as Henry Potter

Richard LeGrand as J. W. Peavy

Charles Cane as Police Chief

Ken Christy as Bailiff

Joan Barclay as Julie Potter

lxiv. Gildersleeve on Broadway, film poster. Public domain.

Gildersleeve on Broadway (1943)

A drug supply company teeters on the edge of closure, potentially leaving Peavey the druggist with no choice but to shut down his beloved shop. Throckmorton Gildersleeve ventures to the bustling metropolis of New York City, driven by his unwavering desire to lend a helping hand. When he arrives, he is warmly embraced by the president of the company, a lonely widow.

Cast

Harold Peary as Throckmorton P. Gildersleeve

Billie Burke as Mrs. Laura Chandler

Claire Carleton as Francine Gray

Richard LeGrand as Mr. Peavey

Freddie Mercer as Leroy Forrester

Margaret Landry as Marjorie Forrester

Lillian Randolph as Birdie

Gildersleeve's Ghost (1944)

Emerging from their resting place in Summerfield cemetery, the apparitions of Jonathan Q. Gildersleeve and Randolph Q. Gildersleeve catch sight of a present-day newspaper headline that reveals the candidacy of their descendant, Throckmorton P. Gildersleeve, for the position of police commissioner. The two apparitions plan to support their relative's campaign by having him reveal the sinister experiments carried out by Dr. John Wells and his assistant, Henry Lennox. Gildy's campaign receives support from various sources, including love-sick newspaper columnist Harriet Morgan and Leroy Forrester, Gildy's nephew. Leroy intends to appeal to animal lovers by donning a gorilla costume.

Cast

Harold Peary as Throckmorton P. Gildersleeve / Ghost of Randolph Q. Gildersleeve / Ghost of Jonathan Q. Gildersleeve

Richard LeGrand as Mr. Peavey

Freddie Mercer as Leroy Forrester

Margie Stewart as Marjorie Forrester

Marie Blake as Harriet Morgan

Emory Parnell as Police Commissioner Haley

Nick Stewart as Chauncey

Frank Reicher as Dr. John Wells

Joseph Vitale as Lennox

Lillian Randolph as Birdie

The Television Series

In 1955, Willard Waterman played the lead role in a television adaptation of *The Great Gildersleeve* series that aired on NBC. This iteration, however, was brief, lasting only thirty-nine episodes. During that year, both the fifteen-minute radio show and the television show were being created concurrently.

In the television series, Throckmorton P. Gildersleeve was portrayed as less endearing, more pompous, and a more overt womanizer. According to Harold Peary, the issue with the television series was that 6'3" Willard Waterman was ill-suited for the role. The character Gildersleeve was a shorter man who had a larger-than-life personality.

Barbara Stuart made her television debut on *The Great Gildersleeve*, portraying the character of Gildersleeve's secretary, Bessie. Child actor Michael Winkelman, who later starred in *The Real McCoys*, also had his television debut on the show, playing the character of nine-year-old Bruce Fuller.

lxv. Willard Waterman as Throckmorton P. Gildersleeve in the television series The Great Gildersleeve. Circa 1955. Public domain.

Cast and Characters

Throckmorton P. Gildersleeve	Willard Waterman
Leroy Forrester	Ronald Keith
	Tim Considine (*1 episode*)
Marjorie Forrester	Stephanie Griffin
Birdie Lee Coggins	Lillian Randolph
Mr. Peavey	Richard Le Grand
	Forrest Lewis
Floyd	Hal Smith
Bessie	Barbara Stuart
Judge Hooker	Earle Ross
	Harry Antrim
Foley	Burt Mustin
Mayor Terwilliger	Willis Bouchey
Lois Kimball	Doris Singleton
Brandon Fuller	Raymond Bailey
Charlie Anderson	Robert Foulk
Eva Jane Wingate	Jean Willes
Vivian Bennett	Mary Costa
Amy Miller	Marian Carr
Mrs. Hogan	Doris Packer

lxvi. Ronald Keith (Leroy) and Willard Waterman on The Great Gildersleeve TV series (1955). Public domain.

lxvii. Stephanie Griffin (Marjorie) on The Great Gildersleeve TV series. Public domain.

Episode Log

EPISODE	TITLE
1	GILDY GOES BROKE
2	PRACTICE WHAT YOU PREACH
3	CIRCUMSTANTIAL EVIDENCE
4	GILDY GOES DIVING
5	GILDY AND THE CON MEN
6	GILDY STEWS ABOUT A COOK
7	GILDY, THE PRIVATE EYE
8	GILDY'S JUVENILE DELINQUENT
9	GILDY, KING OF HEARTS
10	ONE TOO MANY SECRETARIES
11	THE RAFFLE
12	WATER COMMISSIONER'S WATER COLOR
13	THE NIGHTMARE
14	BARD OF SUMMERFIELD
15	GILDY GOES HOLLYWOOD
16	GOLF BALL INCIDENT
17	COMMAND PERFORMANCE
18	THE QUIET ONE
19	ORANGE BLOSSOMS IN SUMMERFIELD
20	THE GOOD SCOUT
21	GILDY AND THE EXPECTANT FATHER
22	GILDY TANGLES WITH LEROY'S TEACHER
23	GILDY LOVES WELL, BUT UNWISELY
24	PROTECTIVE PARENT
25	BIRDIE'S GOLDEN DREAM
26	TWO GIRLS, ONE BIRTHDAY
27	THE WHISTLING BANDIT
28	GILDY'S DANCING LESSONS
29	MARJORIE'S APARTMENT
30	GILDY THE GO-BETWEEN
31	GILDY PULLS THE SWITCH
32	GILDY'S ALL-AMERICAN BOY
33	PRISONER OF LOVE
34	GILDY HIRES AN EAGER BEAVER
35	THE POLITICAL PLUM
36	GILDY'S EFFICIENCY KICK
37	CALLING DR. BERGSTROM

| 38 | THE DEED |
| 39 | BEAUTIES AND THE BEAST |

Trivia

What was the motto of the Gildersleeve Girdle Works?
"If you want a corset, of course it's ... Gildersleeve."

What became of the Gildersleeve Girdle Factory in Wistful Vista?
The factory was converted into a repair shop for zeppelins.

What was the address of the Forrester residence in Summerfield?
747 Parkside Avenue.

What was the name of Marjorie and Leroy's father?
Charles Forrester. He managed a real estate agency and a car dealership.

Where did Leila Ransom live?
Leila and Throckmorton resided on the same street. Leila's address was 269 Parkside Avenue.

What was Judge Hooker's address?
The old goat resided at 2100 Burnside Avenue, three blocks from the Gildersleeve residence.

Where was Floyd's Barber Shop located?
Across the street from Peavey's Pharmacy on State Street.

Where was Peavey's Pharmacy located?
On the corner of State Street and Parkside Avenue.

When did Peavey's Pharmacy open?
It opened in 1921.

What was Peavey's full name?
Richard Quincy Peavey.

Did Mr. Peavey serve in the military?
Yes, he served in the 49th Field Artillery. He commanded a platoon of mules.

What was Mrs. Peavey's maiden name?
It was Horsefall.

What was Judge Hooker's name?
Judge Hooker's name was given as: Horace Greeley Hooker, George Horace Hooker, and Horace W. Hooker

What nicknames did Gildersleeve give the judge?
He sometimes called him "the fury of the jury" and "the stench of the bench." He also called him the "old goat."

What was Police Chief Gates' first name?
It was Donald.

Who was Summerfield's Water Commissioner before Gildersleeve?
Commissioner Clanahan.

Who was the engineer at the Summerfield Water Works?
Charlie Anderson.

What were the names of Bronco's parents?
Edward and Martha Thompson.

What was the name of Bronco's bottled water company?
The Babbling Brook Water Company.

What were the names of Marjorie and Bronco's twins?
They were Ron DeLinn and Ron DeLinda.

What was Summerfield's radio station?
WSUM "The Voice of Summerfield."

What was the name of Summerfield's newspaper?
The Summerfield Indicator-Vindicator.

When was the Jolly Boys Social Club formed?
1943.

Who were the members of the Jolly Boys?
Throckmorton Gildersleeve, Judge Horace Hooker, Police Chief Donald Gates, Richard Peavey, and Floyd Munson.

What was the motto of the Jolly Boys?
"One for all and all for one."

Where did Aunt Hattie live?
Twin Oaks.

Where was Grass Lake located?
125 miles from Summerfield.

What lodge did Birdie belong to?
The Mysterious and Bewildering Order of the Daughters of Cleopatra.

What school did Leroy attend?
He attended the P. J. Fluegelhammer Junior High School.

What was Leroy's friend's name? The one he liked to play pranks with.
His name was Piggy Banks.

What was the name of Summerfield's Haunted House?
It was the Burton Mansion, where it was rumored that the original owner murdered his wife.

Who was the mayor of Summerfield?
Mayor Terwillinger.

Who was the town doctor when the show first aired?
The town doctor was Dr. Sillsby. His telephone number was Rosebud-2212.

Who were the announcers on the program?
They were Jim Bannon (1941-42), Ken Carpenter (1942-45), John Laing (1945-47), John Wald (1947-49), Jay Stewart and Jim Doyle (1949-50).

Who were the writers on the program?
They were Leonard L. Levinson, Gene Stone, John Whedon, Sam Moore, Jack Robinson, John Elliotte, Andy White, Paul West and Virginia Stafford Lynne.

lxviii. The Great Gildersleeve cast photo featuring Judge Hooker, Throckmorton P. Gildersleeve. Marjorie; Leila, Birdie, Leroy and Mr. Peavey. Public domain.

Notable Quotes

Throckmorton P. Gildersleeve—

    "This is going to be one of my baa-aa-aa-aad days!"

    "You're a haa-aa-aa-aard man, McGee!"

Mr. Peavey—

    "Well, now, I wouldn't say that!"

    "I've got a special on nickels today. Five for a quarter."

"A man was in here the other day and asked me if we served eggs. I told him we served everyone."

Police Chief Gates—

    "Fellas! Fellas! Let's all be Jolly Boys."

Leroy Forrester—

    "What a character!"

    "Are you kiddin'?"

    "For corn sake!"

Leila Ransom—

    "Why Thrawk-mahhhhtin..."

Floyd Munson—

    "Slip right into the chair comish!"

List of Photos/Illustrations

i. Mr. and Mrs. Willard Waterman. Circa 1940s. Public domain......................v

ii. Actor Harold Peary best known for his role in The Great Gildersleeve. Circa 1945. Public domain..x

iii. Fibber McGee and Molly with Ted Weems and his orchestra broadcasting from Chicago in 1937. Public domain..6

iv. Jim and Marian Jordan. Circa 1930s. Public domain....................................8

v. Writer Don Quinn. Public domain..16

vi. Jim and Marian Jordan as Fibber McGee and Molly. Fibber's opening the closet and everything falling out was a long-running joke on the radio program. Circa 1948. Public domain...21

vii. Throckmorton P. Gildersleeve and Fibber McGee. Circa 1941. Public domain..22

viii. Cast of The Great Gildersleeve circa 1948 (Seated from left to right: Lillian Randolph, Gloria Holliday, Una Merkel, and Mary Lee Robb. Standing: Richard LeGrand, Earle Ross, Walter Tetley, Harold Peary, Jack Meakin (Musical director), John Wald (Announcer), and Arthur Q. Bryan. Public domain..28

ix. Advertisement for The Great Gildersleeve presented by Kraft. Compliments of Kraft Foods, Inc. 39

x. Harold Peary as the star of The Great Gildersleeve, circa 1940s. Photo by Ernest Bachrach. Public domain. 40

xi. Harold and his first wife, Betty. Public domain. 48

xii. 1946 press photo of Betty Peary, the wife of actor Harold Peary, Beverly Hills. Public domain. 49

xiii. Publicity photo featuring Harold Peary, his wife Gloria, and their son Page Peary. Circa late 1940s. Public domain 50

xiv. Harold Peary and his son Page at Kiddieland. Circa 1952. Public domain. 50

xv. Willard Waterman as Mr. Merriweather in the U.S. television situation comedy The Halls of Ivy. Circa 1950. Public domain. 51

xvi. Willard Waterman and Shirley Mitchell. Circa 1956. Public domain. 52
xvii. Walter Tetley circa 1940. Public domain.. 58
xviii. Walter Tetley performing his Scottish routine. Public domain................ 60
xix. Lurene Tuttle, Dr. Christian publicity photo. Circa 1940. Public domain. 67
xx. Harold Peary, Walter Tetley and Lurene Tuttle publicity photo for The Great Gildersleeve. Public domain. 68
xxi. Leroy, Gildersleeve, and Marjorie (Lurene Tuttle). Circa 1940s. Public domain. 75
xxii. Gildersleeve, Leroy, and Marjorie (Louise Erickson). Circa 1940s. Public domain. 76
xxiii. Mary Lee Robb, early 1940s. Public domain.. 82
xxiv. Walter Tetley, Harold Peary, Mary Lee Robb, and Jeanette Nolan. Public domain. 86
xxv. Gildersleeve gives away the bride from LOOK Magazine May 23, 1950 pictorial feature. Public domain... 87
xxvi. Lillian Randolph on The Beulah Show. Cicra 1952. Public domain. 88
xxvii. Richard Crenna. A Date with Judy. Public domain. 94
xxviii. Arthur Q. Bryan as Floyd Munson the barber, Willard Waterman as Throckmorton P. Gildersleeve and Earle Ross as Judge Hooker on The Great Gildersleeve. Public domain. 100
xxix. Richard LeGrand as Mr. Peavey. Public domain................................... 106
xxx. Richard LeGrand and Harold Peary in Gildersleeve's Ghost (1944). Public domain. 111
xxxi. Forrest Lewis. Circa 1940. Public domain.. 112
xxxii. Arthur Q. Bryan. Circa 1955. Public domain... 116
xxxiii. Shirley Mitchell. Circa 1943. Public domain.. 122
xxxiv. Gildersleeve with Leila and Eve. Circa 1940s. Public domain. 130
xxxv. Cathy Lewis. Public domain... 134
xxxvi. Gale Gordon as Rumson Bullard. Public domain. 139
xxxvii. Gale Gordon and Bea Benaderet Granby's Green Acres 1950. Public domain. 140
xxxviii. Jim Backus and Jone Allison performing on Casey's Girl Friday. Circa 1943. Public domain. 145
xxxix. Jim Backus performing for the NBC Blue Network. Circa 1940s. Public domain. 146

xl. Ken Christy who portrayed Police Chief Gates on The Great Gildersleeve. Circa 1953. Public domain. 153

xli. Katie Lee with Willard Waterman on The Great Gildersleeve. Circa 1948. Public domain. 154

xlii. Harold Peary who portrayed Honest Harold and his wife Gloria Holliday who depicted Gloria the switchboard operator on the Harold Peary Show on CBS. Circa 1951. Public domain. 159

xliii. Harold Peary working on The Harold Peary Show for CBS in 1951. Public domain. 160

xliv. Kathryn Card and Charles Cooper in How to Marry a Millionaire (1957). Public domain. 168

xlv. From left to rightt: Jane Morgan, Robert Rockwell, Gloria McMillan, Richard Crenna, Eve Arden and Gale Gordon from Our Miss Brooks. Public domain. 171

xlvi. Jane Morgan. Public domain. 172

xlvii. CBS publicity photo featuring Gloria Holliday at the information desk. Circa 1944. Public domain. 177

xlviii. Gloria Holliday. Circa 1950. Public domain. 178

xlix. Joseph Kearns. Public domain. 182

l. Joseph Kearns' beloved pipe organ photographed in 1957. 188

li. Situated on the opposite wall from the console, a grill conceals the organ chambers in Kearns' living room. Circa 1957. 189

lii. The Kearns residence circa 1957. 190

liii. Willard Waterman and Parley Baer during a rehearsal for The First Nighter. Circa 1948. Public domain. 191

liv. Parley Bear circa 1940s. Public domain. 192

lv. Willard Waterman, Barbara Luddy and Olan Soule on The First Nighter. Courtesy of Mary Anna Waterman. 196

lvi. Mary Jane Croft. Public domain. 200

lvii. Mary Jane Croft with Hattie McDaniel and Henry Blair on The Beulah Show, Circa 1948. Public domain. 203

lviii. Sammy Ogg, child actor. Circa early 1950s. Public domain. 204

lix. The Great Gildersleeves in New York. Cicra 1977. CC BY-NC-SA 4.0..210

lx. Ad in the Village Voice for The Great Gildersleeves. October 31, 1977...211

lxi. The Great Gildersleeve comic book story. Circa 1944. 214

lxii. The two Gildersleeves, Willard Waterman and Harold Peary, backstage at A Funny Thing Happened on the Way to the Forum.Courtesy of Mary Anna Waterman. 220

lxiii. Lobby card for the 1941 film Look Who's Laughing. Public domain. ... 242

lxiv. Gildersleeve on Broadway, film poster. Public domain 247

lxv. Willard Waterman as Throckmorton P. Gildersleeve in the television series The Great Gildersleeve. Circa 1955. Public domain 251

lxvi. Ronald Keith (Leroy) and Willard Waterman on The Great Gildersleeve TV series (1955). Public domain. 253

lxvii. Stephanie Griffin (Marjorie) on The Great Gildersleeve TV series. Public domain. 254

lxviii. The Great Gildersleeve cast photo featuring Judge Hooker, Throckmorton P. Gildersleeve. Marjorie; Leila, Birdie, Leroy and Mr. Peavey. Public domain. 260

Works Cited

"A Date with Judy." Wikipedia, Wikimedia Foundation, 14 July 2024.

"Actor Richard Crenna Dead at 76." CNN, Cable News Network, 22 Jan. 2003.

"Actor Willard Waterman Dead at 80 - UPI Archives." UPI, UPI, 3 Feb. 1995.

"Arthur Q. Bryan." Wikipedia, Wikimedia Foundation, 27 May 2024.

"Barbara Ruick." Wikipedia, Wikimedia Foundation, 7 Apr. 2024.

Barnes, Mike. "'I Love Lucy' Actress Shirley Mitchell Dies at 94." The Hollywood Reporter, The Hollywood Reporter, 13 Nov. 2013.

Baxter, Devon. "Radio Round-up: Arthur Q. Bryan." RADIO ROUND-UP: Arthur Q. Bryan |, 20 Sept. 2017.

"Bea Benaderet." Wikipedia, Wikimedia Foundation, 19 July 2024.

Beck, Alan. "What Is a Boy?" www.appleseeds.org.

"Cathy Lewis." Wikipedia, Wikimedia Foundation, 10 Feb. 2024.

Cox, Jim. "'Let's All Just Be Jolly Boys!' Well Now, I Wouldn't Say That, Mr. Gildersleeve." Old Time Radio Researchers, 2020.

Davis, Linda. "Ken Christy (1894-1962) - Find a Grave Memorial." Find a Grave.

Dickson, Terry. "Forrest Lewis." Newspapers.Com, St. Louis Post-Dispatch, 1 Sept. 1948.

"Don Quinn." Wikipedia, Wikimedia Foundation, 29 June 2024, en.wikipedia.org/wiki/Don_Quinn.

"Don Quinn Dead; Top Radio Writer; Creator of 'Fibber McGee and Molly,' a 17-Year Hit." The New York Times, The New York Times, 31 Dec. 1967.

FamilySearch.Org, ancestors.familysearch.org/en/LVFW-LPB/donald-f.-quinn-1900-1967.

"Fibber McGee and Molly." Creative Serendipity Memories, 13 Nov. 2014.

"Fibber McGee and Molly." Old Radio World, www.oldradioworld.com/shows/Fibber_McGee_and_Molly.php.

Fibber McGee and Molly," St. James Encyclopedia of Popular Culture. Encyclopedia.Com. 14 Jun. 2024." Encyclopedia.Com, Encyclopedia.com, 30 June 2024.

"Fibber McGee and Molly." Wikipedia, Wikimedia Foundation, 29 June 2024.

"Fifteen Cent-World Radio History." World Radio History, Jan. 1945.

"Forrest Lewis." Wikipedia, Wikimedia Foundation, 24 June 2024.

"Gale Gordon." Radio Hall Of Fame, www.radiohalloffame.com/gale-gordon.

"Gale Gordon." Wikipedia, Wikimedia Foundation, 7 June 2024.

Genzlinger, Neil. "Ben Gazzara, Risk-Taking Actor, Is Dead at 81." The New York Times, The New York Times, 3 Feb. 2012.

Gilliland, Norman. "The Great Willard Waterman." Wisconsin Life, 10 Feb. 2018.

"The Great Gildersleeve." ONESMEDIA, www.onesmedia.com/comedy-c-96_101/the-great-gildersleeve-p-54.html.

"The Great Gildersleeve." Wikipedia, Wikimedia Foundation, 4 June 2024.

"The Great Gildersleeve and the Evolution-Revolution of Comedy." Old Time Radio Shows from the Golden Age of Radio, 10 Apr. 2019.

"'The Great Gildersleeve' on WIBA Today at 4:40." Newspapers.Com, The Capital Times, 31 Aug. 1941.

The Grouch Club." Wikipedia, Wikimedia Foundation, 2 Sept. 2022.

"Harold Peary." Hollywood Walk of Fame, 9 Dec. 2020.

"The Harold Peary Show." Wikipedia, Wikimedia Foundation, 23 Nov. 2023.

"Harold Peary: The Great Gildersleeve and More." Classic Film Aficionados, 24 Jan. 2017.

Harrigan, Tom. "Character Actor Baer Dies at 88." The Napa Valley Register, 24 Nov. 2002.

Hastings, Deborah. "Harold Peary, Star of Radio's 'great Gildersleeve,' 76, Dies." Los Angeles Times, Los Angeles Times, 1 Apr. 1985.

"History of NBC." Wikipedia, Wikimedia Foundation, 6 July 2024.

IMDb. "Kathryn Card - Biography." IMDb, IMDb.com, www.imdb.com/name/nm0136293/bio/?ref_=nm_ov_bio_sm.

"Jane Morgan (Actress)." Wikipedia, Wikimedia Foundation, 20 July 2024.

"Jane Morgan: Radio Star: Old Time Radio Downloads." Jane Morgan | Radio Star | Old Time Radio Downloads.

"Jim Jordan (Actor)." Wikipedia, Wikimedia Foundation, 30 June 2024.

"Irreplaceable Richard Crenna." Legacy.Com, 17 Jan. 2013.

"Jim Backus Collection." Old Time Radio, www.otrcat.com/p/jim-backus.

"Joseph Kearns." Wikipedia, Wikimedia Foundation, 2 Mar. 2024.

"Joseph 'Mr. Wilson' Kearns Doesn't Mind Playing Straight Man to a Child Actor-He Was Once One Himself." *TV Guide*, 15 July 1961.

"Kallmann Syndrome." Wikipedia, Wikimedia Foundation, 29 May 2024.

"Kathryn Card." Wikipedia, Wikimedia Foundation, 18 Mar. 2024.

"Katie Lee (Singer)." Wikipedia, Wikimedia Foundation, 8 July 2024.

"Ken Christy." Wikipedia, Wikimedia Foundation, 20 Mar. 2024.

"Leonard Levinson." Wikipedia, Wikimedia Foundation, 19 Apr. 2024.

"Leonard Levinson, Radio Writer, Dies." The New York Times, The New York Times, 2 Feb. 1974.

"Lillian Randolph." Wikipedia, Wikimedia Foundation, 17 May 2024.

"Louise Erickson (Actress)." Wikipedia, Wikimedia Foundation, 1 Mar. 2024.

"Lurene Tuttle." Wikipedia, Wikimedia Foundation, 20 July 2024.

Lynch, Jacqueline T. "Richard LaGrand - Mr. Peavey and a Film Debut." Richard LaGrand - Mr. Peavey and a Film Debut, 23 May 2024.

"Marian Driscoll Jordan." Wikipedia, Wikimedia Foundation, 29 Apr. 2024.

Martin, Tom. "Katie Lee Remembered." Mountain Buzz, 5 Nov. 2017.

"Mary Cline Obituary (2006) - Palm Springs, CA - The Desert Sun." Legacy.Com, Legacy, 12 Sept. 2006.

"Mary Lee Robb Cline, 80; Played Gildy's Niece on 'the Great Gildersleeve.'" Los Angeles Times, Los Angeles Times, 8 Sept. 2006.

McLeod, Elizabeth. "Afra's First Lady: The Career of Lurene Tuttle." Radio Classics, 29 Aug. 2015.

McLeod, Elizabeth. "Eternal Youth: Walter Tetley, Radio's Essential Kid." RadioSpirits.Com - Walter Tetley, 2012.

McLeod, Elizabeth. "The Great Gildersleeve: Character Counts." Radio Classics, 31 Aug. 2016.

McLeod, Elizabeth. "'Why, Thrawkmawtinnnnnnnn...' The Radio Life of Shirley Mitchell." Radio Classics, 4 Nov. 2016.

Mishkind, Barry. "The Story behind: 'Transcribed.'" The Broadcasters Desktop Resource, 29 Feb. 2024.

Mr. Peavey." Media Heritage - Preserving Radio and Television History, 12 Mar. 2013.

"Olan Soule." Wikipedia, Wikimedia Foundation, 10 May 2024.

Old Time Radio Lovers. "The Great Gildersleeve." Old Time Radio Lovers, 20 Dec. 2019.

Oliver, Myrna. "Olan Soule; Actor's Versatile Voice Led to Multimedia Career." *Los Angeles Times*, Los Angeles Times, 4 Feb. 1994.

"The Only I Love Lucy Cast Members Still Alive Today." Facts Verse, 1 Nov. 2023.

"Parley Baer- Biography." Turner Classic Movies, Turner Classic Movies.

"Parley Baer." Variety, Variety, 26 Nov. 2002.

Peary, 'Great Gildersleeve," Dies at 76, The Milwaukee Journal, 1 Apr. 1985.

Rapaport, Diane. "Katie Lee and Great Gildersleeve." Drapaport's Blog, 2 Mar. 2015.

Richard Legrand." Wikipedia, Wikimedia Foundation, 3 June 2024.

Richard Legrand." Wistful Vista, sites.google.com/site/wistfulvistasite/wistful-vista/fibber-mcgee-and-molly/cast-and-crew/richard-legrand.

Sandomir, Richard. "Katie Lee, Folk Singer Who Fought to Protect a Canyon, Dies at 98." The New York Times, The New York Times, 10 Nov. 2017.

"Shirley Mitchell Famous Death." Khoolood, 6 Nov. 2014.

Shreve, Ivan G. "Happy Birthday, Cathy Lewis!" Radio Classics, 27 Dec. 2021.

Shreve, Ivan G. "Happy Birthday, Don Quinn!" Radio Spirits, 18 Nov. 2018.

Shreve, Ivan G. "Happy Birthday, Earle Ross!" Radio Spirits, 29 Mar. 2019.

Shreve, Ivan G. "Happy Birthday, Harold Peary!" Radio Spirits, 25 July 2003.

Shreve, Ivan G. "Happy Birthday, Jane Morgan!" Radio Spirits, 16 Dec. 2019.

Shreve, Ivan G. "Happy Birthday, Jim Backus!" Radio Spirits, 25 Feb. 2017.

Shreve, Ivan G. "Happy Birthday, Louise Erickson!" Radio Classics, 28 Feb. 2020.

Shreve, Ivan G. "Happy Birthday, Mary Lee Robb!" Radio Spirits, 15 Feb. 2020.

S, Ivan G. "Happy Birthday, Olan Soule!" Radio Spirits, 28 Feb. 2021.

Shreve, Ivan G. "Happy Birthday, Richard Crenna!" Radio Spirits RSS, 30 Nov. 2014.

Shreve, Ivan G. "Happy Birthday, Walter Tetley!" Radio Classics, 2 June 2018.

Shreve, Ivan G. "Happy Birthday, Willard Waterman!" Radio Classics, 29 Aug. 2016.

Smith, Mickey C. "Images of Pharmacy and Pharmacists in Old-Time Radio: A Profile of Richard Q. Peavey." JSTOR, Pharmacy in History, 1983.

Stiles, Jim. "Live! With Katie Lee." Canyon Country Zephyr, 2002.

Stumpf, Charles, and Ben Ohmart. "The Great Gildersleeve." Bear Manor Media, Boalsburg, PA, 2002.

"Tex Avery." Wikipedia, Wikimedia Foundation, 9 June 2024.

"The Rape of Richard Beck." Wikipedia, Wikimedia Foundation, 1 Aug. 2024.

"There Is a Tavern in the Town." Wikipedia, Wikimedia Foundation, 4 July 2024.

Thurgood, Lowell. "Forrest Lewis (1899-1977) - Find a Grave Memorial." Find a Grave, www.findagrave.com/memorial/100622920/forrest-lewis. Accessed 10 Nov. 2024.

"Utah-Born Actor Dies in California at 88." Deseret News, Deseret News, 3 Dec. 2002.

"Victoria: Top Performers Appear in 'No Way Out'." Shamokin News-Dispatch, Newspapers.com, 6 Oct. 1950.

"Walter Tetley." Wikipedia, Wikimedia Foundation, 11 June 2024.

Wartts, Adrienne. "Lillian Randolph (1915-1980)." Black Past, 10 Dec. 2020.

Williams, C.S. "Harold Peary: The Great Gildersleeve and More." Classic Film Aficionados, 24 Jan. 2017.

"Willard Waterman." Wikipedia, Wikimedia Foundation, 6 June 2024.

"Willard Waterman Collection." Old Time Radio, www.otrcat.com/p/willard-waterman. Accessed 19 July 2024.

Williams, Rachelle. "Lillian Randolph: A Prolific Black Actress of the Classic Film and TV Era." Reel Rundown, 15 Mar. 2023.

Yours Truly Johnny Blogger. "Harold Peary's Honest Mistake." The Great Detectives of Old Time Radio, 29 Jan. 1970.

About the Author

Author KRISTINE OHKUBO resides in Los Angeles and writes about Japan and Japanese culture. While growing up in Chicago, she developed a profound respect and love for Japan and its people. She has written extensively about this intriguing nation, drawing on her frequent travels to provide readers with her unique perspective.

She made her publishing debut in 2016 with an anthology of travel blog posts about Japan, which was later revised and republished in 2022. Over the years, she has published numerous books about Japan and its rich culture. Additionally, she has lent her expertise to the production of various publications for fellow writers.

In late 2024, the pursuit that launched her into the world of writing ultimately concluded her literary odyssey. She shifted her focus away from Japan and Japanese culture and returned to her original passion for old-time radio. She published a comprehensive book that detailed the entire history of the popular radio show, *The Great Gildersleeve*. The show was highly successful in the United States during the 1940s. Through this journey, Kristine's writing career came full circle.

As an author, Kristine, believes that exploring different cultural perspectives through writing fosters empathy, understanding, and expands our historical awareness.

www.ingramcontent.com/pod-product-compliance
Lightning Source LLC
LaVergne TN
LVHW061034070526
838201LV00073B/5032